SET THE TONE

Nothing Can Change Until You Do.

SABINE JACKSON

Copyright © 2021 Sabine Jackson

sabinejacksonconsciousliving.com

ISBN

978-0-6451355-0-3 (paperback)

978-0-6451355-1-0 (hardcover)

This work is copyright. Apart from any use permitted under the *Copyright Act 1968*, no part of this publication may be reproduced, stored in a retrieval system or transmitted in any form or by any means, electronic, mechanical, photocopying, recording or otherwise, without the prior written permission of Sabine Jackson.

The Cover Design is by: Creative Offsider

The author photo is by: Simone Markham Photography

Layout and typesetting: Busybird Publishing

For Kassy and Trumpet (Trumpsy),

my four legged angels.

Thank you for the lessons.

My eternal gratitude and love.

Contents

Introduction	1
Chapter 1	9
Planting Seeds	
Chapter 2	21
A Conscious Choice	
Chapter 3	31
The Power of the Pause	
Chapter 4	41
Patterns and Programs – It's a Family Thing	
Chapter 5	55
Creating Space for Change	
Chapter 6	69
Laying the Foundation	
Chapter 7	85
Set the Tone	
Chapter 8	99
When the Critic Becomes a Guide	
Chapter 9	117
Creating New Outcomes	
Chapter 10	131
A Whole New World	
Appendix	147
Suggested Further Reading	163

Introduction

I'm in the single bed in the spare room. Fitting, really, because although I'm married, I feel single. Alone. The bedside lamp is on, emitting a soft, warm light, but I feel anything but soft or warm inside. I feel confused and lost. It's a cold winter's night so I'm wrapped in the doona, lying on my back and staring at the ceiling. I'm in a swirl of confusion. Thoughts are racing around my head and my stomach is churning with a mixture of fear and dread.

I reach for the only thing that feels like a lifeline to a better life: prayer. I start my ritual of asking for help. "God, please help me." I don't say anything more specific because to be totally honest, I have no idea what I want. What I do know, with every fibre of my being, is that I want to feel better. And so, like a stuck record, I just keep repeating the same line over and over again, "God, please help me. God, please help me. God, please help me." Until I finally fall asleep—only to wake to the same feelings in the morning.

And then only to spend another day, week, year thinking, "How did I get here? How did I—a smart, insightful, and often even considered 'wise' young twenty-something woman get to be living a life in which I feel so out of control? How come I can't get my marriage to work? How come I want to leave my job but can't figure out what I want to do instead?"

It wasn't as if I was not proactive about creating change in my life. I wasn't just sitting back, expecting things to magically work out. But no matter how much I tried I just couldn't get the people around me to come to the party.

Case in point...

I'm sitting in the car on the way to the counsellor. I'm nervous about speaking to a stranger but excited that I will soon be vindicated and *Sean will finally understand that he has wronged me. And relieved he'll soon see that he owes me an apology. It feels good to think that after months of fighting—after all the pain and tears—we will finally be able to start repairing our relationship and moving forward.

We arrive at the clinic and take a seat in the waiting room. Even though I know I'm in the right and that the counsellor will spend most of the session explaining to Sean how wrong he's been, I still feel anxious. It's a vulnerable step that he and I are taking.

After what feels like the longest time, the counsellor finally opens her door and calls us in. She sits down in a chair, and Sean and I take our seats opposite her. I'm to her right. "How fitting!" I think to myself.

I begin to tell her what has happened in our relationship. I explain to her that after the offending incident, I broke things

*Name changed for privacy

off but that we have been back together again for the last few months. This is partly due to Sean's pleading but also because I am still in love with him and don't really want the relationship to end.

Then I explain the reason why we are sitting in front of her. "Sean won't apologise for what happened. He refuses to apologise." She listens to me, then listens to Sean. The hour is quickly over, with no resolution, and she asks to see us again the following week.

The next week, as we sit once again in the waiting room, I think to myself, "Okay, this is it. Here we go." As we enter her office, we all take the same seats we sat in the week before. Again, the counsellor listens to me and then to Sean. The whole thing is essentially a repetition of the first session.

This does not lessen my shock when, at the end of our hour, this counsellor woman has the gall to turn to me and say, "He is clearly not going to apologise. You will need to be able to move forward without an apology."

Umm, I'm sorry ... what?! "So," I conclude to myself, "Out of all the counsellors we could have gone to, we clearly found one who is defective and hopeless at her job!" As Sean and I sit silently in the car on the way home, I feel so dejected. If I can't get him to see that he is in the wrong and needs to apologise, how will I be happy in the relationship? I spend the rest of the drive trying to figure out a Plan B.

As I remember this scene now and share it with you, I can see the comedy in it. I can laugh to myself as I imagine the look on my face as the counsellor uttered those words: "You will need to be able to move forward without an apology." Oh, how often I have, in turn, received that same look from clients over the years.

We have all heard the expression, "The only thing that can change is you," but at that time, I simply wasn't ready to really take this in. In fact, it would take over a decade before I was able to recognise this truth.

If you are anything like me, you are well acquainted with the yearning for things to be different. You may be wanting a better relationship, a different career, and/or an improvement in your financial state. Maybe you don't have a clue what you want, but you just know you don't want things to be the way they are now.

I remember that feeling so well. First, I wanted *this* to be different, and then I wanted *that* to be different. As the years rolled on, I eventually came to a feeling of wanting *everything* to be different. Then—surely *then*—I would feel better. I had no idea how to feel better unless the things that made me feel like crap changed. But I also had no idea how to change any of those things because the more I pushed for change—desired it, willed it—the more everything stayed the same. I needed help.

So, that was always my prayer: "Help me!"

"Help me with clarity, help me to feel better, help my relationship to be better, help me to get out of nursing, help me to have more money, help me to not hate my body. Just help me with this pain—this extraordinary, overwhelming pain. And this extraordinary desire for things to be different."

Introduction

And thus, we come full circle, back to my desperate night time pleas to the heavens from that single bed in the spare room on that fateful winter's night.

Now, you might imagine that God answered soon after that night. Maybe in a flash of clarity, I received a simple and easy, ten-step action plan—my very own set of commandments—after which I proceeded to sail smoothly through my thirties. But that, my friends, is not what happened.

And here's why, in a nutshell:

I couldn't get clarity and a direct line to guidance. Although I was constantly pleading, back then, I wasn't actually listening to, or even open to, the guidance that was coming in. In fact, usually, when I was most desperate, I was also the most closed off to relief. Also, in reality, I didn't actually want guidance. I just wanted to feel better, and I wanted things to be 'fixed'—which is vastly different from being open to solutions. What I really wanted was to be plucked from that bed and 'saved.'

Thankfully, the 'me' sitting here today is so glad that this is not how it works. Even if on some days (and even some years), it felt like I took the long way around, I did ultimately figure out how to get myself out of that bed, so to speak. I am glad because, if I had been 'saved' by something or someone other than myself, I would not have the confidence I have today. I wouldn't have the trust in my own ability, the trust in life and the knowing that we live in a benevolent universe—where everything that happens is for our own good. A million lessons would have gone unlearned, and I would have had to go through it all again the next time around (in the next life, which I do believe in).

Plus, I wouldn't have written this book, and you wouldn't have it in your hands. This book is for you. It's for all of us who are pleading for pain to stop, pleading for clarity, pleading for things to be different. I want you to know I see you. I want you to know that I will take you through how to get yourself out of your own proverbial bed. And I'm going to show you why the pleading, the asking, the affirmations, the vision boarding, the yelling, the crying, the begging ... why none of it has worked for you thus far.

Just as I got *my*self out of that place, I'm going to help you get *your*self out. Yes, that's right. *You* are going to do it. This book isn't going to save you, and *I'm* not going to save you. You are very powerfully and lovingly going to save yourself. When you have learned what I'm going to share with you, you can apply it for the rest of your life. Then there will be no more desperate pleading.

Let's take a deep breath of relief, knowing that the guidance has arrived. It's right here—exactly what *you* have been asking for, exactly what *I* was desperately longing to know ...

How can I feel better?

How do I get things to be different?

How do I get things to be the way I want them to be?

While I wrote this book for you, it is actually also, in many ways, a dialogue between my former self and me. I can still see her so clearly — full of attitude. And she is such a great guide to me now. I feel a bit like the ghost of Christmas future from *A*

Christmas Carol, entering the room to tell this former self how to rise and claim her life. In turn, she is the ghost of Christmas past, helping me write this for you. Her questions and her yearning have shaped this book, and it is the lessons learnt that fill its pages.

And what if *you* also already exist in some future time? (Of course, you do—I'm just introducing this topic gently, as I don't want to lose you in the introduction!) And what if that future you is handing the 'present-moment' you this book?

Just imagine, somewhere there is a ＿＿＿＿＿＿＿＿＿＿ (insert your name) already living with clarity, purpose, confidence, and trust.

These pages are here to help you 'catch up' to future you and embrace this way of living.

It's time to rise and claim your life.

Chapter 1

Planting Seeds

*"Without realising who you are,
happiness cannot come to you."*

Yogi Bhajan.

Imagine this ...

Each morning you wake up with a full basket of power, and your ability to access that power is at peak capacity. But a few moments after waking, you realise you are getting out of bed to go to a job you don't like. You feel no ability to leave that job at this time, and you feel you are not going to the job willingly. So, out of your basket of empowerment comes some of your power. It flows out of your basket to everyone and everything you feel has either led you to being in that job or is stopping you from being able to leave. So now you are at, let's say ... 80 percent of your power.

Then you get your kids ready for school, or you battle with your partner for bathroom space. Your sense of frustration heightens. You focus on all the ways you look after your kids and/or your partner and organise them rather than being able to focus on yourself and your own needs. Again, more power flies out of your basket and you are now at 50 percent of what you had when you first woke up. You have 'lost' 50 percent of your power in less than an hour, and you haven't even walked out the door yet! This has all occurred before you've begun interacting with the 'outside' world for the day.

Once you've left your house, you start the drive to work, and you're soon faced with the traffic, the bus that slows you down, the difficulty getting a parking spot, and the recollection that you don't even like this job. In fact, you realise you hate it and can't stand coming here anymore. You do a quick run-through of all the reasons why you are stuck in the job and can't change your situation, and by the time you walk into the building, you are down to about ten percent of the power you woke up with.

So, when the co-worker (who always looks at you like she is judging everything about you) starts to walk over to you and you assume that you are about to have a negative interaction with her, you lose the last little bit of connection you had to your power. You then spend the rest of your day being in a state of triggered responses, feeling like a victim of your circumstances. Each conversation you have reinforces, to yourself and your family and friends, that although you want a different life and do not want to feel this way anymore, there is nothing you can do about it. Not until you can get a different job, get your partner to change, get your kids to be more responsible, get your mother to stop pressuring you, get your sister to start being more supportive ...

You get the picture.

Can you relate to this? I sure can. My own personal experience with this phenomenon was that I felt stuck — stuck in nursing, in a relationship in which I didn't feel heard, in a body that was never perfect enough, and in a whole slew of other relationships and circumstances to which I was unconsciously handing over my power, every single day; whilst at the same time affirming that I could create anything I wanted to.

Why do we do that? How come we can recognise the truth that we are strong and powerful and that we can create a life that we imagine while at the same time be haemorrhaging power left and right and feeling completely victimised by life? The answer to this is quite simple—just one small word: ego.

Yep, it's that concept that people sing about, talk about, accuse people of, are offended by, and use as an insult. And I'd love to tell you that simply learning the true meaning of this one three-letter word will answer all of your questions and completely change your life overnight—that once you understand ego you will never have a worry or a problem again. But of course, that's not the truth.

Here is how it went for me:

When I first ventured into spiritual texts, I found that there were many different names used to refer to the same thing. "Ego" is the word that resonated with me the most but, even so, for many years it was just a concept.

With each encounter, though, through a different teacher or author, I learnt a little more. I understood at a slightly deeper level. However, it wasn't until I read *A Course In Miracles* (ACIM) that it all came together enough for me to start actually living my life with a conscious awareness of ego.

And still, change and even relief didn't come overnight. Does it ever? And let's be honest, if it did, would we be equipped to maintain it? Or would we be like the lotto winner who goes from poverty to being a millionaire and then straight back to poverty in the span of a few short years?

Why can't awareness and relief be instant? You can certainly decide in the blink of an eye and proclaim something like, "I will never do that again," or, "That's the last time I allow_____." And in that moment, you may well mean this affirmation with all of your being. But after the initial emotional surge has calmed down or completely gone away, your mind will go back to its 'autopilot' setting, and your ego will start to pipe up. Long-held beliefs will rear their ugly heads, your ancestral and cultural programming will all kick in again, and your life will start to go back to 'normal.' It's back to business as usual in the world that is you.

Each time this happens, what generally results is that you feel more and more defeated by life and less and less able to create change. Here's the thing with change, though: it can happen in the blink of an eye. Every breath, every thought, every experience is an opportunity for you to do things differently, to choose differently. However, lasting and permanent change doesn't happen from doing things differently just once. It's choosing differently again and again and again. I always say it's about 'choosing better,' each time, and by 'better,' I mean choosing yourself.

To create a foundation for change and to be an open recipient of all that you wish to receive, the starting place must be this understanding:

Planting Seeds

> **One of the main reasons nothing has been changing and you are often times in pain is because you have forgotten who you are.**

The most powerful place to start to teach you how to make better choices is to remind you of who you are. Many of us are completely disconnected from this. I certainly was when I was lying in that spare room bed and pleading for relief. I had no idea of my own power. I knew enough to know that I could ask for help. Still, I had absolutely no idea of my place in the creation of either the 'problems' that I was facing or the solutions that I craved. The pain I was feeling was primarily due to having forgotten myself and having disconnected from my power.

So, who are you? You might be able to answer this quite simply. Your response might contain a lot of titles for what you do. For example, you might say, "I am a teacher," "I am a nurse," "I am an entrepreneur." Or it might contain some of the roles you have in others' lives. For example, you might respond with, "I am a mother," "I am a partner," "I am a sister," or "I am a friend." Or maybe what comes to mind first for you is what you love or are passionate about, such as, "I am an animal lover," "I am a book lover," "I am an artist." These descriptions will vary for each one of us. One that does not vary between us, that applies to every single one of us, and is most easily forgotten is:

> **You are an incredibly powerful being and creator. You are an extension of all there is. You are equipped to create miracles and to transform anything, any experience that you find yourself**

> in, and then use this as material to build yourself up. You have the ability within you to create a foundation that is so solid, so strong it can withstand anything without you losing your sense of self. An experience might make you wobble a bit. Still, with a foundation based on knowing who you are and feeling connected to all there is (and by making decisions from love rather than fear), you cannot be knocked down.

The enormity of this truth may not be fully understood until the end of this book, but we need to at least plant the seed for this understanding now, at the beginning. We need to help you remember who you are and help you reconnect to your power for all of the other lessons in this book to have their full effect. Forgetting ourselves and the power, all we have access to is the single thing that wreaks the most havoc in our lives.

So, here's the seed we are planting, together, for you right now:

> **I always have the power. No one outside of me has any power over me.**

It's a big statement, I know. And Ego will fight it immediately. It will bring to your mind a million examples of when you were legitimately powerless. It will have at the ready a million 'buts' for you to fire at me in response to such a fanciful affirmation.

But when we go through life thinking that something needs to occur or someone needs to start or stop acting a certain way for us to be able to feel the way we want to or accomplish the things we want to, we are handing our power over to those people and conditions. We hand our power over to them on a silver platter and then wait for them to hand it back. By doing this, we have put them in charge of our lives and made ourselves a victim.

At twenty-something, lying in my spare room bed praying for relief, I would totally have responded to everything I am now suggesting to you with, "This does not apply to me. I don't want to be a victim. In fact, I'm a tough, independent woman, and being a victim is the last thing I want!"

Here is what I would say to that version of me now, as well as to you if all this talk of handing over power and choosing to make yourself a victim is triggering you ...

"It's not you, it's Ego."

So, when I'm talking about Ego, what is it that I'm referring to? In Chapter Two, I will fully acquaint you with your ego but for now let's do a quick introduction. The ego is an aspect of our mind that comes along with this human experience. We all have one. Yes, we do. It is the part of our mind that is the least evolved but has the most responsibility for keeping us safe and alive. It, therefore, spends most of its day in a state of fear and anxiety. It doesn't like change because it hates to be out of control. It is small and narrow in its thinking. And it gathers all of its information in order to assess any 'now' moment in relation to the past.

How does your desire for change and craving for a different, better life get received by Ego? With a great deal of fear and reluctance. Not to mention a great many reminders of all the times in the past when you have tried to change and 'failed,' or of times when those around you didn't support your changes.

Ego has no capacity to have insight or to see the bigger picture. Couple this with its desire to keep you safe and here is what it is going to tell you about each situation, relationship, or challenge that you find yourself in:

1). It's someone else's fault.

2). You can't change this. Someone or something else must change before this can be different.

3). You aren't enough, and you don't deserve this (even if this one is not obvious to you, I promise that on some level, it is swirling around in each one of us).

4). Someone else holds a key piece of your puzzle, and until they do a certain thing or until they hand that piece back to you, you cannot live the life you want to live.

Ego wants to ensure that everything stays the same. And this is what has been happening to you. It is also the reason you might be feeling very disheartened and powerless, or angry and frustrated at life and the way it works. By having a fear of being uncomfortable and applying the above beliefs to your life, Ego is ensuring that nothing ever really changes because nothing is changing within you.

What happens instead is that you try to implement change while believing that you have no real power. So things may change for a little while or feel different for a bit, perhaps because you are in a new relationship or a new job. But no profound, lasting

Planting Seeds

change can occur while you have forgotten who you are and you falsely believe that all of your power is in other people's hands. Remember the basket?

Now, be honest. Have you ever thought one, or even all, of the above thoughts? Do you believe that something else needs to be different before you can get the change you want in your life? Before you can feel better, does something outside of you have to happen? Does someone need to enter your life, leave your life, or be different so that you can have what you want or feel the way you want? Or is it you that you feel needs to be different? Are you not enough as you are?

If you answered yes to any of these questions, it is because your ego is telling you this is true, and it has been telling you this for so long that you now believe it to be truth. In this way, you are trying to create change in your life without having access to any feelings of power. No wonder it's not going well. No surprise that you are disheartened. Or maybe you are taking the experience of everything staying the same as evidence of your lack of power?

So far, you haven't achieved the results you want because you have been attempting to create from ego and fear and from an aspect of you that thinks you are a victim and has very little or no power. You have been attempting to create whilst thinking and collecting evidence about life from an aspect of your mind that doesn't want anything to change. Its desire to keep you safe and its addiction to control mean that it wants everything to stay exactly as it is because even if things are painful and completely unlike how you want them to be, at least they are predictable.

17

There is no unknown to navigate; there are no situations or scenarios that your ego can't predict the outcome of and keep you safe from.

This a dream for the ego, because the ego is a control freak—but it's a complete nightmare for the part of you that is programmed to be an expansive being. Your whole purpose for being here is to learn and grow and create, and to experience a bigger and deeper life. The part of you that remembers this is craving something more.

I'd like you to think back to what life was like before your mind became harsh, critical, frightened, and basically a big risk assessment strategist. What happened to the little girl or the little boy you were who was fearless and dreamed big? The little person full of life and inspiration, who looked at the world and was excited to explore and create?

You started out full of love and compassion. You were quick to forgive, and you always spoke your mind. Maybe you can even remember feeling like you could do anything? Whatever you remember of that original state of innocence, strength, possibility, THAT is the real you. That child—the child you are connecting with in your memory and your vision—is closer to who you really are than the person you see before you in the mirror today.

In this moment, reading the above, Ego might be saying, "That was when I was naïve, when I didn't know any better." Ego will try and convince you that you are now living in the real world, the grown-up world where things are hard, and there's no time for daydreaming. Now you have to work and pay the bills. And parent and do all sorts of jobs and chores that you don't want to do. And that's what's real. Your heart has been broken too many times for you to be that little person again. You wouldn't even want to be that innocent and trusting because that would make you vulnerable and unsafe.

However, one of the most significant differences between that child and the woman or man you see in the mirror today is, back then, you didn't give your power away. You could create incredible joy just by being you—by being in the moment, in your body, playing, creating, having fun. Since then, you have started outsourcing for your sense of worth and for your joy. What you have, what you do, and how people treat you has become the gauge of your value.

Do you see yourself as a success? Look around. Do you have 'the' partner? The right house? The right things? Do you have the right clothes? Are you thin enough? Are you liked? Do you have enough friends? Are you happy? Are you in good relationships? Are your children successful? Is your house clean enough? How many 'likes' did your last photo get on Instagram or Facebook? When you did the ten-year profile pic challenge, did people say, "You haven't aged a bit"?

How many of these things do you give power to? What of these things can make you feel good or bad about yourself? Here's the irony. We think we are the grown-ups. We think we are wiser now than when we were that little person who believed in their ability to do anything and be anything, and who believed in the innate goodness of all people and all living things. This couldn't be further from the truth now. As adults, most of us are far more unconscious and disconnected from 'real' life than we were when we were talking to imaginary friends and holding tea parties with our toy animals.

So, what happened?

The truth is NOT that life happened and woke us up out of our fairy-tale perception of the world. The truth is that Ego happened. It started to build and grow and gain a hold over our thinking. Ego began accumulating evidence of 'truth.' Belief systems were programmed and strengthened, and we became more unconscious, more asleep. In this way, the most unevolved part of our mind initiated itself as the louder voice, which produced a constant stream of dialogue. And slowly, you came to believe that that louder voice was you—this could not be further from the truth.

Chapter 2

A Conscious Choice

"Hope and fear cannot occupy the same place.
Invite one to stay."

Dr. Maya Angelou.

Throughout our lives we move between ego and wisdom, fear and love. No one is in one state all the time. When we are in an ego state of mind we are focused on our fears, limitations, what is lacking and missing, and our mistakes. Basically, we are problem-focused. When we are in our wisdom, or our Right Mind[1], we are inspired, expansive, focused on all that we can be, and in gratitude for what we already have. We are essentially solution-focused.

Imagine the freedom, the relief, and sense of power you would feel if you were able to move between these two states all the time. Able to recognise ego and consciously move yourself to your Right Mind each time. This is what it means to be awake, to be aware, to be living consciously. No one is fully awake all the time. We all, and I mean *all*—everyone from Eckart Tolle to your

---

1   Right Mind is the term used in ACIM to refer to the wiser and more connected part of our mind. I like this term as it helps to remind me that when someone is in their ego, they are literally not in their right mind. I interchange the terms Right Mind and Inner Guide.

Auntie Flo—move back and forth between being awake to who we are (in connection with wisdom), and asleep to our power (led by our triggers, fears, misconceptions and judgments).

At this point you might be thinking something like, "Wow, this ego thing is a massive burden! Why on earth do we have one?"

I wondered that myself as I learnt more about the human mind. Or perhaps I should say: as I learnt more about this human experience. At first, I felt immense relief to be able to give a name to the Inner Critic that had been building inside me from childhood. I was also relieved to recognise that this voice, this harsh and judgmental dialogue, was not really me attacking myself. My alleviation, however, was unfortunately short-lived.

After the initial high, I then asked, 'So, what now?' And the two main questions that surfaced for me were: Why do we have an ego, and how do I beat mine into submission? What I discovered over the next 15 years or so of study and self-discovery led me to view the ego as an essential aspect of this human life and a tool for spiritual development.

Picture this scene ...

This scenario is inspired by Michael Newton's book, Destiny of Souls[2].

You are between lives and are getting ready to have a human experience for the purpose of expanding your soul. Before this adventure begins, you go and see a panel of wise beings. You let them know what it is that you want to learn or expand upon in your coming incarnation. Together you choose the perfect

---

2 Michael Newton, PH.D. Destiny of Souls. Llewellyn Publications. 2012.

scenario, and then the 'set designers' get to work, setting it up for you!

If you are already familiar with my work, you will have heard me use the phrase, "Trust the set designers." I say it all the time to remind myself and my clients that everything has been created perfectly and that we can trust the process of life. I'll expand upon this in later chapters.

For now, back to the 'set designers.' Everyone and everything gets to work creating the 'right life' for you. At this stage, you are involved in creating the set and selecting the cast. Loving souls put up their hands to play the support roles. Everything is perfect—except for one thing: If, while living this perfectly created scenario of your life, you remembered exactly who you are, who all the support cast are, and why they are there; if you were connected consciously to your purpose for being in this life, the lessons you wanted to learn, the scenarios you wanted to play out to enable you to evolve—if you remembered everything straight away, none of it would work.

Think of a movie. When you are enthralled in watching a dramatic film, you feel all the emotions right along with the actors. When you are watching a horror or a suspense film, you can be totally freaking out, heart beating fast, sweaty hands, nervous tension all through your body. Then you remind yourself, "It's a movie," and you talk yourself back to a state of calm. You might even laugh at the reaction you just had.

Now imagine if, during every challenge, disagreement, or significant life event, you knew it wasn't 'real.' It just wouldn't work properly. Without your reaction to the planned 'reality,' you wouldn't face the learning experience. To a certain extent, coming to recognise the illusion is our life's work. It is important that we realise that the set designers got it right. That we comprehend the grand design and eventually come to trust that everyone in our life is playing their part. This allows us to gather our material and expand into all that we can be. It truly is our life's work.

But if you already knew all of this when you were coming into this life, it wouldn't work very well. Being in the illusion and then waking up to it is what we work toward. But there does need to be an illusion to wake up from in the first place.

Well, unless you are someone like Jesus. There have clearly been humans walking the earth at various times who have always known exactly who they are as well as the greater purpose of life. Jesus was one of them. Buddha, on the other hand, is an example of a human who woke up fully whilst initially being in the illusion. For sure, some beings come to earth to teach on a mass scale and model to the rest of us. If you are one of those beings, I am honoured that you are reading my book! If you aren't, then the takeaway message is that an ego is a vital part of the experience. Without one, you would not be able to fully participate in this adventure called life. The ego allows us to be in the illusion until we recognise it as such—and even once we do recognise it, we often toggle back and forth. And that is also part of the design.

So, back to the second question in my initial exploration of ego: "How can I beat it into submission?" This question, or some variation thereof, is very common. If we are stuck with this critical and fearful voice, how do we control it or suppress it? How do we show it who is boss? The short answer is: "We don't."

When faced with something unpleasant or confronting in our life, our first response is generally to get rid of it, suppress it or control it. Guess where this response is coming from? EGO! So, you make the assessment that you don't want this ego thing. You no longer want to live with an inner critic. But then you listen to the voice that says, "Tell it to fuck off!" You think, "Oh, that's a good idea! Totally badass and totally in control. Nothing will help me get rid of my ego quicker than if I tell it to shut up, go away, you're an idiot, you have no idea, I'm not listening to you anymore!"

Have you ever tried any of these sage measures? How did they work for you? Did they work for a little while? Usually, what happens when you first start this line of response is that the voice does quiet down. Just like a naughty child who is used to running wild, if you tell the ego to sit down and shut up, it will do so temporarily. Even if just out of the shock of seeing you respond to it that way for the first time.

But after a while, that response doesn't work anymore. You need to up the level of threat. This will work with a child for a certain period of time, but then the child will call your bluff and act out again. After the initial quiet and the feeling of power you get from being able to shut your ego up, just as with the child, you will have to keep upping the ante. So now, instead of your ego putting you down, you are putting your ego down. You are still living in conflict. Your inner world is still harsh and critical.

And news flash ... Ego gets off on conflict. Conflict, fear, and drama are like crack cocaine to your ego. And if you stay here, you are feeding it exactly what it needs to grow and grow and grow. The very thing you think is taking away its power is making it multiply in size. Having your ego yell at itself is, sadly, not even remotely effective in the long run.

The only approach that actually brings permanent relief and freedom starts with remembering that there is a very clear and distinct YOU that is separate from the inner ego dialogue (calling it your inner critic might help you relate). You may not be very familiar with this other version of *you* because Ego has been so loud and has been left unchecked for so many years that you think it *is* you.

It's not. YOU are a very distinct and separate energy from both your ego and your Right Mind. If you weren't, you wouldn't be able to move from one to the other, even unconsciously. This is the time to recognise that, in each moment, you get to choose: Ego or Right Mind, fear or love. Which will you fuel?

A visual that has always helped me imagine this concept is an old steam train. Picture the giant furnace in the engine room. To move the train along, someone had to shovel coals into the furnace. Imagine if your mind worked in the same way. Two furnaces: one marked Ego/Fear, the other Right Mind/Love. And every thought, belief, or action is coal that is stoking one or the other of the furnaces, determining which direction you go in.

See yourself shovelling fuel into the furnace, see the steam rising and the flames burning higher and hotter. Grab a pen and paper and write this down:

> **'Knowing that all of my thoughts, beliefs, and actions are fuelling either the fire of fear or the fire of love, I now consciously choose to fuel love.'**

So, there you are in the engine room of your mind, moving toward something you are excited about. Maybe it's a gathering, an interview for a job you really want, a date with someone you really like, or your first day at a new job. Which furnace will you stoke? Will you consciously be propelling yourself where you want to go, or subconsciously setting yourself off in the wrong direction?

When I held my first-ever talk at my Kinesiology clinic, I had a very profound experience that I recognised immediately as being ego-based. As usual, without any prior prep, I put the call out to see what interest there might be around a series of talks called Mindful Living. I received a very positive response, so I thought, "Okay, yes, that sounds like something clients would really benefit from, so I will do that at some point." I was happy to leave it at that because, although I was excited and inspired to share the teachings, I was not excited and inspired to stand up in front of a group and speak. That is something that has always made me quite nervous.

After about a month, Mr. Cookson, my husband, said, "Are you going to make a date for these talks, or just talk about doing them?" Yes, well, the former option would seem the next logical step. So, I made it official and posted dates for the four talks. There was a great response, and people started to book in. Now here is where the excitement can begin to turn to fear. And, of course, it did. Whilst being happy about the number of participants that were booking in, I was at the same time getting more and more nervous.

This is a normal human reaction. Anyone who has ever performed in front of an audience or run a workshop or class of some kind will be able to relate. It is not unusual to experience the conflicting feelings of wanting a great turn-out while also hoping that no one comes!

On the night of the talk, I was all ready to go. I had set up the room, had long finished writing the content, and done a few practise run-throughs. Then, as I was looking in the mirror, getting ready, I heard a voice say, "And what are you going to teach them that they don't already know?"

Now, cast your mind back to the engine room of the steam train. The furnace marked 'Ego/Fear' was already burning intensely with all the fear and nerves I felt. The one marked 'Right Mind/ Love,' which had inspired me to do the talks in the first place, was, by this stage, almost out of fuel. You know that feeling just before you are about to do something that you have been really excited about, but now that you are facing the reality of doing it, if someone offered to make it all go away, you would happily take them up on the offer? That someone, suggesting you take the 'out,' is Ego.

And it was my ego that piped up that night and decided to remind me of my worst fear: what if they already know all of this and think to themselves, "What the hell am I here for?" Fortunately, I quickly recognised this voice as Ego's. I knew that how I responded in that moment would either stoke the already-heaving furnace of fear or reignite the slowly dying fire of inspiration. I chose to respond in a way that would encourage the latter. The whole situation was already challenging enough, without me not fully supporting myself through it. So, I looked at myself in the mirror and said, "You are going to do a fabulous job, and everyone will be glad they came."

I then sat in my chair in the space I had prepared for the workshop, and I took a few deep breaths. I connected with the joy that I often feel when I connect other people with insights and help them to live more mindfully. When I was able to feel calm and relaxed in my own chair, I sat in every single participant's chair, smiled, and thought to myself, "This is so interesting. I could listen to this talk all day!" Can you sense the changes that my actions made in the furnaces of the engine? Can you see the fire now growing in the one marked Right Mind/Love? Can you feel the burn of Ego/Fear subsiding?

This is the choice that you have in every situation. Knowing you are constantly fuelling one or the other, which will you choose? Can you see how any fear, conflict, doubt, or drama fuels the fire of your ego? If I had responded to my ego that night by saying, "Shut up!" I might have felt a little better in the moment, but I would still have been shovelling coal into the wrong furnace. Instead of feeling calmer and more confident by the fourth talk, I would have just had to up the ante on beating down my fear.

Years later, one of the participants from that first night said to me, "You know, I still have notes from that talk, and occasionally, I look over them again." Wow! What a great example of the truth that we never know what effect we have on someone, and why it is so important not to let our fear get in the way of our inspiration.

Even when you become aware of all of this, and you stop fuelling the ego, these judgments, these harsh and critical words, don't magically go away. And here is where people often want the quick fix that just plain doesn't exist. The truth of the matter is that what you have had playing on a repeat loop in your mind is not suddenly and magically going to go away. But the good news is that when you live consciously, each moment becomes a choice. Each experience is an opportunity to choose.

Chapter 3

The Power of the Pause

"There are no circumstances around you more powerful than the power within you."

Iyanla Vanzant

The gate opens and it's the postman. Lovely man, friendly, always has a spring in his step. Our fairly, newly arrived and still-settling-in pooch, Kassy, springs to attention, barking at the top of her lungs. As she has not reacted this way to other visitors, I am confused and frankly, annoyed.

What can I say? Barking dogs irritate me. The noise is jarring to my nervous system. Even just a few seconds of it, and I'm literally ready for a Valium and a lie-down. So, THIS is not okay. But over the next few months, I begin to notice a pattern around the barking. It only happens when the visitor has a high-visibility vest on. Anyone else can come to the door, ring the bell, come inside, and Kassy is happy and calm. But if she catches a glimpse of a shiny, brightly coloured vest when the postman drops off a parcel or the meter reader walks around the side of the house, she has an all-guns-blazing reaction. I need to find a solution to this problem. Fast.

Wanting to respect whatever feelings are setting her off, be it fear or a desire to protect, I know not to overreact to her reaction. You know what I mean. We've all witnessed it: the barking dog with the screaming owner, which sets the dog off twice as much, so the owner screams even more loudly. I didn't want a competition to see who could outbark whom. And most importantly, I didn't want her to just be quiet because she was more frightened of me than whatever a high-visibility vest represented to her.

I always want my dogs to communicate with me and, of course, to warn me or anyone else in the house if we are, indeed, in danger. But that was just it, right there: we were not, in fact, in danger! So, I realised that I needed to teach her that these people in the shiny vests were allowed on the property. Why? Because I said so.

Here is the solution we figured out together over time ...

I knew my dog would stop feeling like she must protect me from the serial killer postman that came to the door when she understood that I was capable of protecting myself and I would also protect her. In order for this to happen, she needed to know that I knew someone was at the door. She also had to realise that I had assessed them and deemed us safe. Then—and this is an essential part—I had to communicate to her, "I've got this, you can just relax." And I had to do all of this without shouting, "SHUT UP!!!" Because someone shouting, "shut up" most definitely does not 'have this.' In fact, if they ever had 'it,' they have now lost 'it'!

Once I recognised her pattern—the standing up, the straight tail, the low growl—I knew what was coming next: the bark! So, what I started to do when I was out of the room and she barked at one of these people, is walk up to her, pat her on the head, and say, "Good girl. Thanks for letting me know." This was a nice, calm reaction, so she immediately brought her own less-calm response down a notch. If I was in the room with her when someone opened the gate, and I saw her stand up and start to stiffen her body, then I had the opportunity to intervene before she reacted any further.

So, the new scenario now goes like this: the gate opens, and a person wearing a high-vis vest walks in. Kassy stands up from her bed, sticks her nose right up against the window, and her body starts to stiffen. This is my cue! I walk up to the window with great gusto and big energy. I move her out of the way a little by placing my leg between her and the window. I stand next to her with my arms on my hips and stare out the window. She looks up at me with a surprised look on her face, and I can tell that our dynamic is changing.

She is starting to see me as the animal in charge. And this is not because I can get her to shut up and not bark but because she can tell that I'm taking the danger seriously and assessing the situation. Every part of me is communicating to her, "I've got this."

After a few instances of her witnessing this reaction from me, less and less intervention was needed. The gate would click, the meter reader would walk in, and without rising from her bed, Kassy would look out the window. Then I would say, "I see them; they are allowed." And she would go back to sleep, even while the person was still in the garden. Her reaction became less and less pronounced each time we had a high-vis-vest visitor until all she needed was a look at me and a nod indicating, "We are okay," and all was again well in her world. She felt safe and secure, knowing that I 'had' this.

This is how I first started to learn about the power of the pause.

It is ironic that dogs, who actually have no ego, are nonetheless such great illustrations of what our ego goes through. Dogs are sometimes scary looking; some of them have big sharp teeth that could certainly do a lot of damage to someone. Because of this, people often use them to protect, guard and help them feel safe. Many dogs rise to this challenge, either because they love their humans and want to protect them, because they have been trained to behave this way, or because they are scared.

This is exactly the same as Ego. In its protective role, it is constantly on the lookout for danger. And quite often, just like Kassy with the postman, Ego doesn't get it right. One of the main reasons our ego 'fails' is because it assesses danger based on previous programming stored in our DNA and beliefs. This stored programming has been handed down from our parents, ancestors, and society in general, so is not always pertinent to our situation.

When you live unconsciously, your ego feels like, "No one is home, so I better look after the whole house." In a way, your ego has deemed you incompetent and has therefore taken over the full-time job of looking after EVERYTHING! This leads to both you and your ego feeling anxious, overwhelmed, and out of your depth, hoping that no one will ever come to 'the door' and that you can just sit on the couch and be safe.

Here is what I have to say to you about that: Please, for the love of all things holy, take the lead! Take control, walk up to the window, and say, "I've got this."

The pause that I recognised within the chain of events in Kassy's reaction to the situation allowed me to change the entire dynamic. And it allowed her to feel safe. I became the adult who assessed the level of reaction that was needed in each situation. The same thing happens with our ego. As we move through our day, we have the opportunity to choose our responses to each and every situation. We can decide to rise above unconscious, programmed, and triggered reactions by recognising that we can insert a pause.

At first, the window of opportunity to insert a pause before a reaction will be very short. The most powerful way to start to remind yourself to consciously insert this pause is through your breath. If something happens and you begin to feel disempowered or angry, maybe tears spring to your eyes or you have a gut reaction ... BREATHE. Take a deep breath. This will literally separate YOU from Ego. This can be the difference between activating an outdated program that keeps you stuck and gaining a moment of clarity—an opportunity to reach for something new, better, healthier, and more empowered.

This is not about disrespecting or ignoring your feelings. I'm all about respecting how you feel, but I'm also all about YOU reacting (or, even better, responding) rather than letting your ego take the reins. The difference will be huge!

If you let your ego lead for you, the reaction will come from fear, and the decisions it makes will be the 'safe' options. Your ego will always choose maximum comfort and minimal pain. This generally leads to a life with minimal reward and minimal growth. Eventually, it will also result in a life with minimal joy.

To activate the power of the Pause:

- Breathe.

- Say to yourself, "I've got this." By doing so, you are letting Ego know that you are the adult in the room. From here on out, you will be choosing the responses to situations based on how you feel right now, the results you have been getting so far, and the results you want to have.

- Be gentle with your ego as it arises. It's only doing its job. It is simply responding the best way it knows how in order to keep you safe, and to keep itself safe.

- Respect your feelings at all times. Respect the reaction that has gotten through to the keeper. And simply begin to be more aware and more awake to the feeling of the difference between Ego and Right Mind, between Fear and Love.

Although some spiritual teachings focus on moving beyond the ego, I have come to believe that it can play a significant role in our spiritual evolution. Not only can we learn to consciously move from our ego to our Right Mind (and therefore from our critic to our guide), but the critic can become a guide.

We didn't all come here to be spiritual masters. To live in a cave in the Himalayas, meditating 20 hours a day and sleeping on a rock the other four hours. We came here to be humans. To create into matter what we had imagined, and then play the part that perfectly suits the lessons we planned to learn. Remember, trust the set designers!

So, if you are currently floating in the lotus position and you have moved beyond your ego, then I applaud you. But if like me, you are a soul having a human experience, trying to live on purpose and get through the muck without getting lost in victimhood. All while avoiding being weighed down by the often-dense heaviness of this experience. Then I say this to you:

"You have an Ego. Embrace it, learn to live with it, understand it and factor it into your ongoing experience. Get rid of all thoughts of beating it into submission and start to lead it instead."

Once you have practiced inserting a pause, how do you move from the Inner Critic to the Inner Guide? How do you even recognise that you can move from stoking one fire to the other? How do you actually start to move from fear to love?

Here is a scenario that in one way or another we can all relate to ...

You are 18 years old, your best friend has just gotten her driver's licence, and she pulls up in front of your house in a red convertible. It's a sunny day with a clear blue sky and a warm breeze. Your friend is beaming with excitement as she invites you to go for a drive along an ocean road. You get all excited, too, picturing the two of you zooming down the coastline, singing along to your favourite songs with your hair blowing in the wind.

But your mum looks out the window and is having a heart attack in response to this suggestion. She can already see the car crashing and you and your friend dead in a ditch. She might even see herself at the funeral before you have even agreed to go on the drive with your friend.

If you check in with your mum, her face will tell you everything she feels, i.e., DO NOT GET INTO THAT CAR! And that, my friend, is precisely what your ego does to pretty much all of the things you feel excited about and want to enjoy. So, just as an exercise, take Mum out of this scenario and then take your friend out as well. Simply leave the desires and feelings where they are. This all exists within you. There is an aspect of you that wants to expand, have adventures, and feel the complete freedom of following your heart. Then there is the part of you that is frightened about your safety (especially the risk of being hurt by other people), and it says, "Can't we just keep things as they are?"

When you are living unconsciously, the desire for safety and the fear of change is much stronger than the desire for change, growth, and expansion. Ego's voice is the loudest one in your head and so it forms most of the mental chatter in there. Right Mind doesn't often get a word in, except occasionally when you have a strong feeling of inspiration or a clear desire for something specific.

But then you, figuratively, check for the expression on your mum's face. When you see the look of concern there, you doubt that inspiration or idea. Mum's face is a metaphorical stand-in for ALL of our familial and societal conditioning. And once you see the concern there, you hear Ego say, "I don't think this is a good idea." And generally, you will wait for the idea to pass. And of course, it does pass. The problem is, the more often you do this, the greater the consequences. You can't keep ignoring your 'gut' feelings and your 'heart's' desires without some fallout. Often the hints that this suppression of inspiration, desires, and intuition is taking its toll first appear in the form of feelings of anxiety and/or depression. This can eventually even lead to physical illness.

The solution here is to shift out of this unconscious, ego-based autopilot living. To stop allowing fear and lack to run the show. Fear can only create more fear. Lack can only create more lack.

Think about the times when you have been talking to someone who is frightened about something. You are trying to bring some logic into the conversation and give them some advice. Are they open to it? Do they listen? Generally not. The more frightened they are, the more set they are in their opinion. And the more closed off they are to receive or hear anything other than what they have already decided is the truth.

Think about your own desire for change and to feel better. Where is your focus? Is it from a place of what is missing and what there isn't enough of? Are you frightened that nothing will ever change, or that it might be worse if it does? Does it feel safe to change your mind? Does it feel safe to be vulnerable? Can you give people a chance to be different? Can you allow your relationships to completely transform? Can you trust your ability to learn something new? Can you trust your own judgement?

Re-read the previous paragraph and mentally answer the questions as you are reading through it. What insight do you get from your answers? Are you focussing on lack? Are you feeling unsafe? Do you lack trust in yourself to make good decisions? If you answered yes to any of these, then you are stuck in fear and creating from ego. You are trying to create the life of your dreams with the part of your mind that is stuck in the past, addicted to drama, and hell-bent on keeping you safe, i.e., exactly where you currently are.

You see, your ego has done a risk assessment of your current place in life. It has taken stock of your current feelings and your sense of self—and it has decided that you can survive your current circumstances. However, there is a big part of you that wants to do more than just survive and that is why you feel unhappy or unfulfilled with life as it currently is. After all, your soul doesn't just want to survive, it wants to thrive, to soar!

If you are caught in ego, stuck in fear and overwhelm, you cannot access guidance from your Right Mind. The aspect of yourself that is patiently waiting to guide you with compassion, understanding, and love is being hindered by Ego. It is suppressing the part of you that wants to ride in the convertible with the wind in your hair, shouting 'WOOHOO!'; the part of you that tells you there is more, and that you ARE more!

It's time to allow the Right Mind to be your guiding voice.

Chapter 4

Patterns and Programs –
It's a Family Thing

*"You cannot go back and change the
beginning, but you can start where you are and
change the ending."*

C.S. Lewis

Have you ever wondered how your Inner Critic knows just what to say to you? How does it know exactly what will bring maximum impact at just the right time? How does it always know precisely what buttons to push? If you still think that you are alone in how you feel, or that feelings of fear, doubt, shame, and judgement are unusual, let me reassure you that they are experienced by every single one of us.

Each time I describe to a client what their inner critic is saying to them, they are shocked at how accurately I can recreate the conversations in their head. How do I know what their thoughts are? Well, it's very simple. I'm very familiar with and aware of my own thoughts—and I am clear about which ones come from Ego. Also, having worked directly with people throughout my adult life, I have come to understand how universal our thoughts and fears are.

There are, however, specifics that are personal to each of us. This is because each of our individual egos has been programmed by the people around us. So, although our ego has the universal role of keeping us safe and alive, what that means explicitly to each one of us can be quite different. The nuances and specific wording that your ego will use—how it knows just what to say to you for maximum impact at exactly the right time—is uniquely designed for the mind in which it resides. How does this happen?

Cue the family ...

Just as a child grows and develops, so too does the ego. As the child watches, mimics, and learns, so does the ego. The most formative years for this learning and development are from birth to age seven. All of the information gathered in those first years of life—most of it absorbed from our parents—gets stored 'on file.' This information then forms a good majority of the belief system we operate from as an adult.

When we enter this life and begin to explore our world, we have no expectations or preconceived ideas of any of the things we encounter. It is the people around us, our significant carers, who begin the process of passing on information.

What is good? What is bad? What is right? What is wrong? When I do this, what happens? Ego takes all of this in to fulfil its desire to make the world safe and predictable.

If your family is anything like mine, you received many messages and a lot of modelling around what NOT to do and how NOT to live your life. And if, like me, you always had a sense that 'this is not the way it's meant to be,' it can be quite distressing to now be told that everything you observed was being taken in by your ego. And much of your subconscious patterning is causing a repeat of what you purposefully did not want to recreate.

Thinking that we will not be like a particular family member or carry on a family pattern is not enough to change it. But here is the good news (which at this point you may be needing):

1). You are not a victim to this process.

2). You can become conscious of what is in your files, throw out what doesn't work for you, and 'update' them with new evidence. In this way, you can create new beliefs.

3). Your ego is only a tiny part of your mind. You have a whole other, potent part that can help you in this process.

4). This work is part of your purpose in this life. Whatever you help to 'upgrade' benefits the whole ancestral family lineage.

5). This is profoundly fundamental work for truly transforming your mind. You have just found the missing key to why, in the past, change hasn't been lasting.

6). I'm going to walk you through exactly how to do this.

Let me expand on these six points:

Recognising the ego's whole subconscious programming can be alarming. Especially when we realise just how much impact our early childhood had on us—and how much of our minds and beliefs are moulded by our parents to this day. This awareness can also be frightening as a parent.

Whether you are focusing on your experience as the child, the parent, or both, just remind yourself of what was covered in the previous chapter. You are always in the perfect set of circumstances for your evolution. And that evolution is what we are all here for. Remember, trust the set designers.

You could think of familial patterning and inherited beliefs in this way ...

Consider a family home—a big old house that has been in your family for generations (let's say, perhaps, even 14 generations). Each time a family member comes of age, that family member receives the house: to live in, to raise their family in, and most importantly, to renovate as they choose.

The time has now come for you to take over the house. You watched your parents live in it before you. And although they fixed the heating, updated the flooring and added a family room, you always felt that they just didn't do with it what they could have. They didn't bring it to its full potential.

But now it's your turn, and you are going to bring this grand old dame into the twenty-first century. You are going to renovate this house like it's never been renovated before. Previous generations will line the streets and throw you a parade—so in awe will they be at seeing what you've done with the place.

You start the first few years of your adult life full of hope. You take ownership with great gusto, but about five years into the house project, something troubling starts to occur. No matter how much you have tried to deny it, your partner reminds you far more of one of your parents than you are comfortable admitting. And you hear yourself saying things to your kids that you heard when you were a child. You spend most of your time broke and tired, and renovating is the last thing on your mind.

There is also this heavy feeling of being limited and weighed down by something you can't quite put your finger on. But you're certain that if you could figure out what it is, you would feel a lot better, a lot lighter.

Let's unpack this metaphor ...

The 'house' is your ancestral energy. It encompasses all the programs, the patterns, and the limiting beliefs that have been handed down in your family from one generation to the next. Each generation, although consciously desiring to do things 'their' way, unconsciously carries a large filing cabinet of conditioning along with them. It's in their DNA, in their minds, and in their energy fields. Once again, this might be leaving you with a heavy feeling. You may be wondering how to move beyond all of this programming?

Let me remind you of the scenario I described in Chapter Two and the Set Designers we are now familiar with. The family you have (the ancestral lineage that comes with your people) and the 'set' you are in all combines to produce the perfect energy to encourage you to transform.

I promise that all that you have experienced—is the exact material you need to evolve, transform, and alchemise into your gold.

It might feel like you have been 'cursed' or burdened by having an ego programmed by your parents, grandparents, siblings, and society. But evolution can't work any other way. We need to be immersed in our family's energy, and then we do our part to move that energy forward—to expand it.

When we move from fear to love and from judgment to compassion, we are 'renovating the house' from limitation to expansion. Even if you come from a very loving and conscious family and are inspired by your parents, you are still here to expand and transform the energy you've received. This is not about judgment—it's about finding what doesn't work anymore. You can't live a new life from old, outdated beliefs. Especially once you recognise they aren't even truly yours and they could be keeping you from the things you desire.

Now seems the perfect time to share some empowering truths. Your ego, the part of you that has been programmed, is only a small part of your mind. By unpacking it, looking at the files of programmed information, and clearing out what you don't want to keep, you are preparing your mind for deep and lasting change!

Why is it so fundamental to become aware of the ego and its programs in order to create change in your life? Because these belief systems—programmed, filed, and stored many years ago—still, to this day, act like a filter through which you experience life. Therefore, all your perceptions are influenced by your beliefs.

We can relate this concept to 'seeing through rose-coloured glasses,' meaning to see only the good in everything and everyone. Someone who sees the world through rose-coloured glasses doesn't necessarily see things as they are. Instead, they have beliefs that cause them to see things skewed toward the positive.

Each of us has our own individual and unique pair of 'glasses' on. The lenses are clouded with our beliefs and we see everything through those lenses. Once we hold a belief, we can only experience life that way. Our glasses are on, and our perception is skewed in favour of the opinion we already have. Dr. Wayne Dyer said, "You will see it when you believe it." What a powerful reminder.

When we hold a belief, our ego will ensure that we are always proven right. What's more, the Universe, in accordance with the Law of Attraction, will bring us experiences, things, and people who will match our expectations. Let's say, for example, you hold this belief: 'No one listens to me; I am not heard.' This belief plays on a subconscious loop in your mind, and your ego goes looking for evidence to prove you right. Ego then stores that evidence in what I call your 'mental filing cabinet.'

As you go about your days, weeks, and years, you will have numerous encounters at home, at work, with your friends, and with strangers on the street. You will find tons of supporting evidence in these interactions to back up your beliefs.

Ego will highlight any situation in which someone doesn't listen to you to ensure that you are aware of it. Then it will file it away, mentally and emotionally, with similar experiences for future reference. Suppose your belief about not being heard is brought into question. Your ego will have lots of examples on hand as evidence to support it. You aren't just 'making this up'—it is your daily, consistent experience.

And how were these beliefs formed in the first place? They were filed away in your early childhood, each time you observed what was going on around you. As you were watching and listening, your ego was filing away information. Information it would later use to answer questions such as: "Who am I?" "Is it safe?" "Am I loved?" "Am I worthy?" "Am I smart?" "Am I pretty?" "What does it mean to be a boy or a man, a woman or a girl?" "What does it mean to be a grown-up, to have the colour of skin that I have, to be the nationality I am?"

This is when we start to look to the outside world for our sense of self and for acceptance. I have lost count of the number of times clients have told me that they were very intuitive and felt divinely guided as children but then closed those channels off. They closed them off because being intuitive or connected to Source wasn't accepted in their family. Or because they were laughed at by their peers or family members for being 'weird.'

This is a perfect example of a child's authentic, genuine nature being suppressed by their own ego. Yes, the family judged and reacted negatively, but it was the ego that took this appraisal on as a valid judgement and a permanent reaction. Many years later, in adulthood, the ego still assumes and prepares for the same response from everyone you encounter. The ego decides—full stop! And that full stop is permanent and final unless you change your mind. Only you can do that and remove that full stop.

Most beliefs, like the one above, are based on real experiences that were the truth at one point in time. What your ego does, however, is interpret these experiences as permanent. Then, when you encounter experiences that match your already-held belief, they become further evidence and reinforcement for that belief.

What was your school experience like? Did you have trouble learning to read or spell? Did a teacher make a comment that made you feel embarrassed or ashamed? Were you compared to other kids and made to feel like you weren't up to standard? In anything, not just reading. For some of us, it's sport or art or maths. And for still others, the area of comparison and perceived shortfall is social, i.e., how easily—or not—we could make friends.

At some point, we have all had an experience at school that we are still carrying today. Why? Not necessarily because it's the truth but because it's stored in our mental filing cabinet. The adult who still says, "I'm not very good at making friends," has catalogued plenty of observational data to draw from. Or, the person who took it as truth that they weren't very good at reading simply because that idea hasn't been challenged since the ego decided it was a fact and filed it when they were 6 years old.

These experiences, once filed away, form the basis of our perception. Remember the rose-coloured glasses? Well, the pieces of 'evidence' that have been safely filed by your ego about what is 'true' or 'false' about yourself, form the unique 'glasses' through which you now experience life. This is important for you to understand BEFORE you can change any part of your experience. These glasses, which you are not even aware that you have on, are affecting the way you 'see' and feel in any situation you encounter.

Have you ever been in a situation with someone only to have them react in a way that baffles you? Has a friend relayed a story to a third party about a situation you were both in and you thought, "That didn't happen that way at all?" Think about a time when you were on the receiving end of someone's reaction that you felt was completely off or out of proportion. This would be a time when you felt like this person completely misunderstood either what you said or the intention behind it. I'm sure you can think of many such moments.

These are perfect example of the ego in action and how it allows the past to cloud the perception of the present. Consider the story of Grace's relationship issues with her partner, below.

When Grace was growing up, her dad was rarely there. When he was home, he was working or trying to relax and didn't want to be disturbed. So, Grace's reality included a father who was distant, emotionally unavailable, and too tired and stressed to spend time with her. Spending time with his daughter was not his priority, nor were her feelings. His priorities were working and providing for the family.

In its quest to gather as much information as it could in order to keep her safe, Grace's ego was watching and observing. And it came up with these conclusions about her dad:

- I am not important to my dad.

- My dad does not love me as much as he loves his work.

Patterns and Programs – It's a Family Thing

- Spending time with me or listening to me is annoying for my dad and stresses him out.

Once Grace's ego drew these conclusions, it took them as truth — FULL STOP. They then became beliefs. Ego set up a file in Grace's mental filing cabinet and labelled it, 'How My Father Feels About Me.' Now, Grace's ego has a full-time job of proving itself right, and it goes looking for further evidence to support these beliefs.

Each piece of 'evidence' cements the belief and Grace now looks through a filter of perception that is 'clouded' by this belief. She can no longer experience her relationship with her dad in any other way—unless she consciously takes the filter off. 'My feelings aren't important to my dad' is now a lens over her perception that affects how she sees her father. And her ego will not allow the possibility that it is wrong. Because if it does, it has failed at its job to protect Grace from risk and vulnerability.

So now Grace's father is set in her mind in this particular way. Now that in itself would be limiting enough, but unfortunately, her ego doesn't stop there. Ego takes Grace through her days as she goes to school, and as she becomes more aware of boys, and it is armed with the job of keeping her safe throughout all of this. It wants to predict outcomes, to be one step ahead so that Grace is never vulnerable, embarrassed, laughed at, or rejected. Each time Grace is faced with a situation she hasn't been in before, her ego is busily going through its files to determine what the situation means.

As Grace starts to enter relationships with boys, her ego goes looking for information on how to keep her safe in this area of her life. It immediately goes back to the file on her dad as that's the closest information it has about how boys/men will treat her. It copies all of the evidence in that file over to a file labelled 'What I Know About Men In Relationships' (the other file it will rely on for information is the one that stores all that she saw and experienced about how her parents related to each other, as well as what she heard them say about relationships in general). In Grace's mind, her dad now starts to represent all boys and all men, and she gets another new lens placed over her perception as she moves forward in life. This lens filters her experience through these generalised beliefs:

- I am not important to my partner.

- My partner does not love me as much as he loves his work.

- Spending time with me or listening to me is annoying for my partner and stresses him out.

Now cue Ego, looking for the evidence to support these beliefs, with a complete refusal to ever be wrong. And yet again, it is 'FULL STOP'— Grace's future relationship experiences are somewhat of a done deal based on these beliefs and filters. And that is how you get to the current moment on this present day, with Grace standing in the kitchen crying and yelling at her partner. She exclaims, "I never feel like I'm important to you, and I know you don't really want to spend time with me. You just do it because you feel you have to!" And her partner looks at her completely baffled and thinks, "WTF!?"

Of course, Grace came into the relationship already holding these beliefs, with her ego having already decided (even if

Patterns and Programs – It's a Family Thing

she wasn't aware of the decision) that this is how men would ALWAYS treat her. Can you relate to this? Have you entered a relationship with so much hope that this one would be different? Thinking that this person is not like your other partners and they totally get you. And you have finally found someone that is not going to disregard your feelings.

Until that one day, when they do 'disregard your feelings' (from your perspective), and you are the one standing in the kitchen yelling, "you always…" or "you never…" And they are thinking, "WTF?" because this is the first time anything like this has come up. But it certainly doesn't feel like the first time for you. You feel like you have been on the receiving end of this for a lifetime. And now your ego is telling you this person is just like all the other people, sending you off into a spiral of hopelessness that 'it will always be this way.'

Grace's story illustrates how an experience that may once have been true, and the valid feelings that came out of it, become programmed into you as permanent truths and set states of reality. It also shows how beliefs can be outdated and no longer work for you. They may be working to keep you safe in the eyes of your ego, but they are stopping you from being able to experience change in your outer world and in your perception of others. This leaves us only ever living in the past.

Every day, our ego brings the past into the present to help us decide what something means. How can anything ever change while we live our lives in this way? Until you allow things to be different, you are living in a never-ending Groundhog Day. The players change, the words are slightly different, you keep looking older in the pictures, but the feelings and the outcomes are the same.

Does this help you to understand how grown-ups can have tantrums? How an adult who holds down a responsible job and puts on a power suit to go to work every day can have a meltdown like a three-year-old when she finds out a group of friends met for coffee without her? Can you begin to see where your reactions are based on the past?

In these moments, something has triggered the ego, and when that happens, we respond from the age that we were when this issue had its greatest effect. So, we can pout, yell, cry, or throw things. I have several clients who are eye-rollers. Once they become aware of it, we always get a good laugh out of the reaction, and it instantly helps them connect with their power, their Right Mind and 'adult' self again. But it's a great example of what happens when our ego is left to its own devices, i.e., when we are unconscious about our reactions. It will flourish and run the show like a three-year-old with ADD!

So, let's get clearing! It's time to get conscious of what is in your files. I'll walk you through how to 'delete' a lot of the evidence that is outdated, limiting, and not serving you.

Let's begin the most liberating spring clean of your life!

Chapter 5

Creating Space for Change

*"To change yourself is an act of courage and
wisdom. To change anyone else is impossible."*

Martha Beck

How does it feel for you to let go of things? Do you find it
challenging even if you want the change? It's your ego that holds
on. With its focus on lack and scarcity, the ego will generally feel
a sense of anxiety at letting anything go. This is true even if the
thing you're trying to let go of is hindering you, or even if it's
toxic. Ego also wants to make sure that you hold onto proof
and evidence of what it perceives as truth so that you aren't left
floundering and vulnerable.

Just breathe for a moment now and check-in with how it feels
to 'clear out' the mental storage. Is there reluctance around this?
Do you have a feeling of fear or even perhaps an instinct to reject
this whole process downright? When I take clients through this
work, oftentimes they come up against a resistance to answering
questions about their childhood experiences. Some clients don't
want to revisit the past. Others find it confronting to connect
their beliefs with those of their parents.

55

A client once said to me, "I don't want to open that Pandora's box. What if I fall apart and can't continue to live the way I do, holding everything together and keeping on going no matter how I feel?" This is a totally valid question. What this client was really asking was, "What if I go down into the stuff and I get stuck there? What if I remember things or find things there that are so overwhelming or heavy that I break down?"

It is completely understandable to experience fear around bringing what is in the 'dark,' or in your subconscious, into the 'light,' or into your awareness. However, you do not have to stay 'down' there, and you won't get stuck. This whole journey is actually designed to free you and unburden you, not to keep you in an ever-deeper pool of muck. It's also important to recognise that just because you aren't consciously aware of something doesn't mean it isn't having a powerful influence. So you might as well do some excavation since that subconscious stuff is affecting you, anyway, right?

If you are someone who thinks things like, "The past is best left in the past," "I don't want to open Pandora's box," or "What's the point of rehashing the past?"—or if you are very focused on the future and think, "Just focus on where you are going"— you might like to know that these thoughts are actually coming from your ego.

Also, it's worth noting that the point of this exercise isn't to relive the past but rather to understand your mind. This work is about understanding why your ego has come to some of the conclusions that it has come to, and therefore why you hold some of the beliefs you do. When we respect our past experiences and look at them through the eyes of compassion and understanding, we can be free of their hold on us.

Because here is the thing: whatever is in your 'Pandora's box' is still influencing you, no matter how much you suppress it. In fact, I believe that the more you suppress it, the more havoc it causes in your life. It will rear its ugly head in the form of anxiety, depression, and/or physical illness. And it does this so you CAN deal with it. Your higher self knows that you came here precisely to learn from this experience. So, if your go-to is, "While I don't think about it, I'm safe," you're fooling yourself. Because the truth is actually more like this: "While I don't think about it, I stay tied to it and powerless to its effect."

By doing this exercise, you will be accessing the programs that are running through your ego. Let me remind you why it's so important to access this, because you might still be thinking, "I know what my beliefs are, and they aren't working against me." All of the 'evidence' that your mind has gathered is stored up. Even while you may have been thinking to yourself something like, "I will not live like this. I disagree with what is being said," the stored-up 'evidence' has a deep impact regardless of your conscious intention. Even if you aren't aware of it, this is the stuff that triggers you and determines your reactions and decisions.

So, let's proceed gently, knowing that this is an empowering activity. It can only lead to freedom to be more authentically yourself and to expand and evolve the way you live your life.

Grab yourself a pen and some paper or a journal. It's ideal (but not absolutely necessary) to have something that is specially dedicated to this work and then you can write down your insights and add to them at any time (we are going to continue to work with these insights throughout the rest of the book).

*Read through the full instructions before starting.

Here are the main categories that I want to cover, but you can add any that you feel are relevant. You can include any area of your life that doesn't feel the way you want it to or in which the experiences you are having are the opposite of what you would like. Write these headings, one to a page:

- Girls/Women
- Boys/Men
- Relationships
- Friendships
- Work/Career
- Body/Health/Fitness
- Money
- My Role in the Family

Now, under each of these headings, write down what comes to mind. Concentrate on what you saw in your home growing up (especially in the early years up to around age seven) on this topic. What did you hear your parents say about this topic, what was the kind of language used, what was modelled to you?

For the first category of Girls/Women, you would first write "Mum" and then write all that comes to mind about how you heard your mum speak about girls and women. Be sure to write down the kind of words she used. And of course, the most important piece here is: how did she speak about herself and to herself? How did she behave toward herself? She is the most powerful and influential woman in your life. She will give you the most powerful messages about being female and about being a woman that you can receive. Don't just write down what was said—also write down behaviour. As children, we are much more affected by what we see than what we hear.

Next, you would write "Dad" and then do the same exercise for him. How did your dad speak about girls or women? How did he treat them? How did he speak to and treat your mum, your sisters (if relevant), his female relatives, the women he worked with?

Remember, if you had other influential caregivers who had a major role in your upbringing up until around age ten, you'll want to include them as well. This might be a grandparent, aunt, or uncle. If someone comes to mind, trust that and include them.

Continue this process for each category with each parent and/or key caregiver.

Here are some guideline questions for each category in case you need some prompts. If you don't need them, just trust what comes to mind and write it all down. You can always look over this section to see if there is anything else that the questions bring up for you.

The way I have structured these prompts is not going to apply to everyone's family. Some of you may not have had a mum or a dad living with you. Or you may have two mums or two dads. Use the guide and tailor it to your circumstance. Trust your instinct on how best to answer these questions and on what is important for you. I have placed Mum first in each category, but if you are a man, then please put Dad's response in each category first. This is not to imply that both parents or caretakers don't have a powerful impact on our lives, simply that the same-sex parent or guardian generally has the greatest effect on our sense of self and our role in the world at an early age.

- **Relationships** — Categorise into Mum and Dad and consider:

  How did they speak about each other? How did they relate to each other? Did they thrive in the relationship, or did the relationship stunt them in some way? How did they speak about relationships in general? How did they feel about each other? What was their reaction when the other one entered the house or the room? How did they act on holidays? Did they choose to spend time together or keep a lot of distance from each other? Did they touch each other? Were they affectionate? How did each of them speak about other couples? If there were couples, they spoke negatively about, what was it that they focused on about that couple? If there were couples that they spoke positively about, what was it that they focused on in those discussions?

- **Friendships** — Categorise into Mum and Dad and ask yourself:

  Did you see them spend time with friends? You can look at this for each parent individually in terms of their separate friendships, and then also extend it out to friends they had together as a couple. How did they speak about their friends? Were they open or did they tend to keep 'private' things to themselves? How did they speak about and act toward *your* friends when you were a child? Were you encouraged to bring friends home? Were they welcomed? Did your parents value friendship? What did they seem most to appreciate about their friends? Or what did they complain about most? (Remember, you are doing this separately for Mum and for Dad.)

- **Work/Career** — Categorise into Mum and Dad and consider:

  How did Mum talk about work (both her own work and work in general)? About women working? About men working? Were there any differences in your parents' expectations of the kind of work that each gender did or should do? Was some work considered women's work and some men's? Was one kind of work more important than the other down the gender divide? How did each parent speak to you about work? What was the response when you were little and talked about what you wanted to do when you grew up? Remember to go through these questions for Mum, for Dad, and for any other key caregivers in your childhood.

- **Body/Health/Fitness** — Consider:

  How did your Mum talk about her body? What words did she use? How did she talk about women's bodies? (You may already have covered this in the section about girls/women but if you haven't you can include it here.) What about her health? Did she prioritise it? Was exercise and moving her body for

61

fun or wellbeing something that she did? How did she talk to you about sport at school or women in sport? What was her experience with sport at school like? Was she connected to her body and how it felt?

Next, run through these same questions for Dad.

- **Money** — Consider:

  How did your mum talk about money? How did she feel about money? When your mum and dad talked about money, what was the mood like? Did your mum make any money? Was she free to spend it? How did she act around money or bills? Now ask the same questions for your dad. With this category, it's also a good idea to spend some time thinking about your parent's or other caregiver's relationship with money as a couple, and as individuals. Who paid the bills? Who tended to have the major say in how money was spent? Did you have money as a child? Were you given an allowance, or did you sometimes get money as a Christmas or birthday gift? How did Mum advise you about money? How about Dad?

- **My role in the family:**

  This category will give you a lot of insight into your *current* life. There is no need to categorise here. Just write whatever comes to mind—for example, "Peacekeeper, to look after everyone ..." Think of your family as a group and then think and feel into what the messages were when you were a small child in terms of your role in the family. Again, prioritise the messages from Mum and Dad but include grandparents, siblings, and other family members.

Once you have finished filling in each category, what do you do with the information in front of you? I want you to get a highlighter and, as you read back over what you have written, highlight every time you come across something that is the same as or similar to what you currently experience. Also mark up anything you would like to be different, that you want to change.

Here are some examples of what I mean ...

Consciously, you want to create an equal and loving relationship with your partner. Still, your ego is convinced that, just like your dad, 'Eventually all men leave.' Therefore, you hold back and don't fully commit until your partner proves to you that he won't leave. Which of course, he can't convince your ego of, so it's a losing proposition.

Consciously, you want to earn more money. You affirm, you create a vision board, and you get clear with your goals and your intentions. But your ego has been programmed by your mother's voice, saying over and over again that there is never enough money. The dread she experienced every time she opened a bill is still stored in your memory, as are the fights that your parents had about money. You have also started to have thoughts like, "I hate money. Money is the biggest problem in our house." And now, as an adult, you might be saying and doing all the right things but still not drawing any more money into your life.

You started a business you love but can't seem to make any money. Even though you have gone to every business workshop and worked with a business coach for the last six months, you have no idea why it's not going better than it is. There really is no reason. Except now you look over what you have written, you notice that right there in the Work/Career part is your dad saying, "Make sure you get a stable and safe job, so you always know exactly how much money is coming in." And there is nothing stable or safe about working for yourself.

Essentially you are looking through your writing (and your life) for what DOESN'T support what you want to create. Or what DOESN'T encourage the life you want to be experiencing. Once you have the highlighted information in each category, start a new page. Head it with that category, and now just write in the highlighted insights.

For example:

You are doing the category of Money, so you start by writing Money at the head of a fresh page. Then you write down all the things you highlighted about money from the exercise. For example:

- Not enough of it.
- Tension around it.
- Men make more than women.
- Women should prioritise their partner or home life.
- People like us don't have a lot of money.

These highlighted items represent what you saw, heard, or were taught. And, they are in total opposition to what you now want to be living as your truth.

Now look at what you have written for each category from the highlighted items, and write on each of these new pages:

"These are just things I witnessed. They are not THE truth; they are not MY truth. I am willing to change my mind on this and experience a different reality."

Then, I want you to write out the belief that you want to experience and get evidence of. For example:

I easily attract money into my life, I always have enough of it.

Or you might start by writing down the beliefs that you consciously hold, or *want* to hold, in each category and then go looking for evidence to the contrary. Find, amongst the 'evidence' sitting before you, anything that does not support your ideal.

For example, imagine you wish to experience the reality of '*I now enjoy a loving and connected relationship with my partner.*' Keep this in mind and look at everything you highlighted that does not match this statement. Write it down under the heading "Relationship." Then again, write, "These are just things I witnessed. They are not THE truth; they are not MY truth. I am willing to change my mind on this and experience a different truth."

Do this for each category.

What you now have before you are the thoughts, feelings, and beliefs that you may or may not have been aware of. Regardless of your level of awareness around them, they are determining your experience of the world. In a sense, you are now looking at your 'house.' And you can clearly see where that 'house' needs renovating. If you come from a lineage of women who have forgotten their power, then now is your time to remember yours.

65

And you get to leave a sparkly set of tools in the house for the next generation of women to use. They'll be there from the time they enter. As a result, these girls will have the opportunity to be more connected to their power than you once were. (Remember to go easy on yourself if this triggers you. You were taught to be disconnected. It's not your 'fault.')

Did you have a dad, or perhaps a whole lineage of men, who were disconnected from their emotions (who suppressed them and modelled to you to do the same)? If so, now is the time to use the information before you and begin expanding and evolving it. Firstly, recognise that it is not THE truth. It may be someone's truth, but it is not yours. At least it doesn't have to be if you don't want it to be.

If you have been yearning for all of your relationships to be more mutual, heathier, and more conscious, then you now have all the 'evidence' in front of you to clarify what has been standing in your way.

Now is the time to move beyond the ego that is holding the reins and instead, take them for YOURSELF. This whole exercise is a powerful practice. You may wish to do it a few times, or over the span of a couple of days as memories start to come you. Never be afraid of this process. See it as no different from going through the fridge and throwing out all the things that are past the use-by date, have gone off, or are wilted and limp in the back of the crisper.

Be excited with your discoveries. These insights are your golden nuggets on the path to creating new outcomes. It's time to step up and take charge of the incoming information, the processing of that information, and your outgoing responses. In order for all of this to occur, you need to create the right environment. This will give you access to your Right Mind and allow it to guide you. Your inner world needs to switch from fear to love.

Let's create an environment in which you can thrive.

Chapter 6

Laying the Foundation

"As long as man stands in his own way, everything seems to be in his way."

Ralph Waldo Emerson

About four years after I was lying in my spare-room bed, desperately praying for relief and deeply confused as to why all my efforts were not bringing the outcomes I wanted, I had a huge lightbulb moment.

I was sitting on the bed, again in the spare room, and my partner at the time was standing in the doorway. I wouldn't say we were arguing because it takes two people to have an argument. It would be more accurate to say that I was ranting, and he was staring at me silently. I don't remember the exact thing that had set off my rant. Still, I do remember his silence and my feeling of being unsupported.

I felt like whenever I needed him, he ran out on me—not physically but emotionally. I felt that I couldn't reach him. Suddenly, I had a moment of clarity as I realised that I had been doing this same thing to MYSELF my whole life. Whenever I needed myself, I was out of there!

If I were to do the exercise outlined in the previous chapter and think back to how emotions were dealt with in my family home, it would be clear that this behaviour is exactly what was modelled to me. I learned from my parents that emotions are to be disregarded and hidden away as much as possible. They are to be punched or hit away, yelled away, drunk away, smoked away — stuffed down in one way or another. As low as they could possibly go. They were never regarded, respected, or dealt with. So, this was the subconscious belief that was still running into adulthood and was the basis for my reactions.

This is a powerful example of how you can't change something that you aren't conscious of. All these years, I had been wondering why this lack of regard for my feelings came up repeatedly. Not just in romantic relationships but in friendships, within my family, and even at work. A lack of emotional support was my regular experience.

The awareness that I had been withholding—from myself—both emotional support and a sense of regard, was my first foundational shift. This was to become my understanding of the power of 'setting the tone.' And was my earliest understanding of what I now know to be two fundamental lessons in creating change: a) you can't attract what you aren't a match to, and b) you can't thrive in a hostile environment.

I want you to think about what you want in your life. What causes you the most pain or disappointment in your relationships? What do people withhold from you that is painful not to receive? In what way do people predominantly treat you that is hurtful or disregards you? If I were a fairy godmother and showed up right now with my wand and said, "You can have one wish that will transform how all of your relationships feel," what would you wish for?

Once you know your answer to this question, write it down in your journal.

Now, look at what you have written and ask yourself whether you give this very thing to yourself. To be crystal clear, this is NOT about whether you give it to other people, but rather whether you provide it to yourself. Whatever you are withholding from yourself is the only thing truly missing in your life. At some stage, it may have been genuinely withheld from you. When I was a child, I was very genuinely not regarded, nor were my feelings respected. Your feelings and beliefs have a valid starting point, however, what you are now withholding from yourself cannot be filled by anything or anyone outside of you until you have the capacity to receive it. Only then will you be a vibrational match to it.

To be able to receive support, I needed to have a place for that support to land. Otherwise, I was literally incapable of receiving it. People may well have been trying to give it to me, but I couldn't even recognise it most of the time. Other times I did recognise it. But it made me feel so uncomfortable I ran away from it as fast as I could.

One of the most striking examples of this pattern in my life was during the acute stages of recovering from a debilitating back injury. At the time, I lived on my own on the second floor of a block of flats. Every time I needed to get groceries, I had to carry the bags up two flights of stairs. This was okay before the injury but was one of my biggest challenges afterwards, as carrying even a light bag was extremely painful.

One day I arrived home after having been to the supermarket with my brother. After I parked the car across the road from my building, I opened the back door, grabbed the two bags of groceries I had bought, and proceeded to walk toward my building. Completely lost in my own world, I heard a voice say, "Um would you like me to carry those?" I will always remember the massive jolt I had when I realised that I had forgotten that my brother could help me! I was used to doing things on my own. I had become so accustomed to living out my belief that support was scarce, that I literally could not see that support was, in fact, walking right next to me.

How often had I done that? How often had my beliefs clouded my perception so much that I literally could only see the world the way I thought it was? How much did this affect my experience of life and the people around me? Massively. Think about what you may have missed in your life by believing things to be one way and not seeing any different? Where has your ego put full stops on the end of beliefs? Where are you now living out these 'truths,' even though they completely go against what you wish to be experiencing?

Of course, not all of my experiences of being alone and not supported were an illusion. I had plenty of people in my life who really were distant, emotionally unavailable, and selfish. At the time, I took this personally, and it was often hurtful. But the truth of the matter was that I was trying to have relationships and friendships with people who were simply incapable of providing the kind of support I was looking for. This was kind of perfect if you think about it. Because at the time, I was simply incapable of receiving the kind of support I was looking for.

This is a Catch-22 that we can all find ourselves in at various points in our lives. The thing that must shift first, the one who must lead the change, is you! The reason the experiences I was having kept showing up was because they were a 'match' to my belief. At the time, I was truly incapable of experiencing life any other way. Wanting things to be different and knowing what kind of relationships I desired wasn't enough to create the change.

If you are reading this book, I would say there is a high probability that you are familiar with the Law of Attraction (LOA). And even if you aren't, I want to clear up a few things about this Law. If not properly understood, you might not be manifesting what you want and assuming you aren't doing it right. Or, even worse, believing that you aren't worthy of receiving what you want. You might conclude that some force—God, the Universe, Source—has deemed you unworthy.

You may have learnt that The LOA allows you to manifest anything if you want it badly enough. Just create the right vision board, affirm what you want a few times a day, and watch the cash, the love, the dream job, the holidays, the shoes, the cups of tea (okay, maybe that's just me?) all come directly to you. Right? Wrong! If this is your understanding of the LOA, then you may well be feeling despondent. Let me give you a crash course in the Law and get you back on track to creating consciously.

You are always attracting experiences, things, and people to you. Every thought, belief, feeling, and action has an energetic frequency. A particular vibration. Life works so that all things that have the same or similar frequency are attracted to each other. Not drawn together in an after-three-drinks-on-a-Tinder-date kind of way but attracted in a two-magnets kind of way. This process of attraction just occurs naturally.

There is no judge and jury. No one listening to what you wish and pray for, then delivering it to your door by the morning. No one is judging who deserves what or who wants something badly enough. There is no force in place that's moving things around and delivering them to the 'right' people. (More on this along with further context in Chapter 7.)

Here is a striking example of where an incomplete understanding of attraction can work against us: It involves teaching children about Santa Claus. I've come to realise that this well-meaning tradition has a lot of consequences. Think about it. We teach children that a white-bearded man who lives in a fantastical place far away, watches us all year. If we are good, we get what we wish for; if we are bad, we don't. If you were brought up in a traditionally religious home, you may well have been taught the same thing about God. As though God is Santa for adults. The good get rewarded, the bad get punished.

Imagine instead, if kids realised that they get the gifts their parents can afford. Or those that are appropriate for where they live (for example the child who wants a horse and lives on acreage is a lot more likely to get it than the kid who lives in the inner city). Or, they get the gift that is age appropriate. Being taught these things could free children from concluding that when they don't get what they ask for, they are not 'good enough.' Such an erroneous conclusion creates a belief. Although beliefs are generally programmed into us quite subtly, we often carry them for the rest of our lives.

So, it's no surprise that even now as an adult, you may believe (consciously or unconsciously) that if you were 'good enough' and worthy, you should be able to attract everything you want into your life. The child who is taught, 'If you are good, you will get the toy you want,' or, 'If you behave and do all the right things you will be rewarded,' can easily become the grown-up who believes, 'If I were good enough my partner would treat me better,' or, 'If I were thin enough, sexy enough, beautiful enough ... my partner wouldn't have cheated.'

We can falsely believe that not being enough, or being unworthy, is the reason for anything negative that happens to us—from not having the partner we want, to having a miscarriage, to getting cancer. And none of this is true! You are enough. You are an extension of all that is. You are a part of the fabric that makes up the whole universe. Not only are you a part of all that is, you are a vital part of it. Every single one of us is. Yes, we are also human. And when we have forgotten who we are, when fear has taken hold of us, we can speak and behave in ways that aren't fabulous, but no one is actually judging or punishing that.

So, back to the LOA. Like attracts like. As such, we would be wise to keep in mind one of the most powerful lessons from preeminent LOA teacher, Abraham-Hicks. This teaching reminds us that we don't attract what we want, but instead we attract what we are. So, how could I attract support into my life when I wasn't a match to it (because I wasn't being supportive to myself)? If support is missing in my life in relationship to myself, I will attract from outside of me, exactly the same thing: a lack of support.

Now, this part can get a little confusing, so stay with me.

Was I of support to others? Yes, in fact, far too much and at too high a cost. But support was lacking within me. I was not carrying a vibration of support that would make me a match to receiving it. In fact, my lack of support toward myself, together with my beliefs, created supporting evidence in a bulging 'file.' And my thoughts about the 'truth' of all of this was making me a super powerful attractor to more 'lack' of support. Any change that was going to be experienced had to start with me.

Whatever unwanted experiences you are attracting into your life (be it disrespect, disregard, rejection ... whatever it is), it's not because you are 'less than' or not worthy. It's because somewhere in your mind, your beliefs, thoughts, and choices are a match to that. Somewhere along the way, you have picked up unhelpful beliefs and the evidence for them is now playing out in your outside world. How do you stop that from showing up again and again? You start by changing your mind, and therefore, your inner world.

If you look back over the 'beliefs' exercise that you did in the previous chapter, you have laid out before you the evidence that your ego goes looking to support. Your journal is now like your mental filing cabinet put down on paper. These things are still affecting your experience of life, even though you may consciously be trying to live a different truth. How you see and experience the world is filtered through these beliefs. Remember, it's our job to take this information and use it to renovate the house—to expand beyond the programmed beliefs.

To do this, we need to consciously and actively learn to identify when we see evidence of the past and recognise that it is NOT a permanent truth. Just as you have written at the bottom of each category in the previous exercise, "This is not THE truth, this is not MY truth, I am willing to change my mind. I am willing to see things differently." I now want you to say these same things in your mind every time you experience 'evidence' of something you actually want to change.

I'll clarify this by explaining first what I don't mean. I don't mean you should stay in a situation where there is abuse. I don't mean stay passive. I don't mean don't act. I don't mean don't speak out when you feel compelled to. My intention with this exercise is to get you to insert the pause so you can step into YOU. Remember the power of putting in a pause between action and reaction?

By taking a breath and saying, "I am willing to change my mind on this," or, "I don't know what this means," you start to shift from the FULL STOP, done-deal world that ego keeps you in. You can begin to move from where everything is a repeat of the past. And you move into the space between Ego and Right Mind, where you recognise that for real change to occur, you will have to start stoking the 'fire' of your Inner Guide.

You start off by stating to yourself, "I don't know what this means." That gives you just enough time to shift the energy. If I take you back to the example of my dog, Kassy, and the men in high-vis vests coming through our front gate. Kassy represents my ego. She sees that gate open, catches a glimpse of high-vis, decides we are in danger, and goes into full protection mode. By standing up and moving toward the window to check the situation out myself, I insert the pause. This is like you saying to your ego, "Hang on, I'm going to check this out myself." Because you aren't yet able to recognise when ego is acting, and therefore stop the trigger (or the unconscious reaction) before it occurs, you start by saying, "I don't know what this means."

This allows a stop-gap between Ego taking over and telling you what it means. It tells you things like, "It's because he doesn't love me"; "It's because she doesn't care"; "It's because they think I'm stupid"; "It's because they take me for granted" and on and on. None of these assumptions are helpful. They may well be the truth, but if anyone should decide that, you want it to be you and your Inner Guide, not your ego.

None of this is meant to imply that you aren't being disrespected or that your assessment of a situation isn't correct. But we want you to be the one making that decision and then deciding how to respond, rather than your ego being in charge.

Also, when you assess a situation through your automatic filters, without any conscious input from your Right Mind, Ego will always make everything be about you. And the truth of the matter is, so very little about someone else's reactions, choices, language, and behaviour is ever about you. By convincing us that everything is about us, and being done to us on purpose, Ego keeps us in constant states of reactivity. Constantly bouncing from one trigger to another. It will have us convinced not only that we are victims to everyone else's 'poor' behaviour and choices, but it will also use their behaviour to beat us up!

You know the drill ... someone treats you badly, you feel like crap, and you ask yourself, "Why would they do that?" Then you get upset—maybe frustrated or even angry. And when the heightened emotions wear off, you turn on yourself and decide you are the idiot for letting them 'do it to you' again. But YOU aren't doing any of that. Your ego is doing it. You are the sleeping bystander, watching it as though you have no control. Ego's voice is the loudest voice in your inner dialogue, so you think it is you—or even worse, you think it's some higher guidance.

What you see as abuse occurring outside of you now becomes abuse within you—from you to you. Or, more accurately, it is from Ego to Ego. It essentially argues back and forth with itself. Using the 'evidence' you collect about others against you. You end up beating yourself up with anything you can get your hands on.

Many of us are such harsh critics of ourselves that our internal worlds are like a war zone. This is because we have let our ego run our mind, unchecked. And this has significant repercussions on our inner world. We are looking for worthiness in the outside world while ruling our inner world like a dictator. We can't thrive in an environment like that. We can survive, but we can't thrive. The relationship we have with ourselves is the basis for every experience across our life. Not only is it the most important relationship we are ever in, but it sets the tone for all other relationships we have.

At this point I would like you to get your journal out and write in nice big letters:

Why should anyone else treat me better than I treat myself?

Imagine this ...

(If you are a man reading this, substitute the little girl in this story for a little boy.)

Your friend arrives at your door with her five-year-old daughter—a girl whom you have loved since the day she was born. You adore spending time with this child. Your friend asks you to look after her daughter for the day, as she has been unexpectantly called into work.

You are about to say, "Yes, of course," when you hear a voice say ...

"If you say 'yes,' you can only speak to this little girl the way you talk to yourself. The whole day, anything you would typically say to yourself, she will hear about herself. How you would normally look at your body and feel about it, she will feel. What you usually feed yourself, she will also be fed. How you normally respond to your own emotions, will be the way she feels hers responded to.

Laying the Foundation

You look back at her mother's expectant face. Do you:

A. Say, "Sure, bring her in."

OR

B. Tell her to run like hell and slam the door shut as quickly as you can?

If you answered b), thank you for your honesty.

I want this to be the gauge you now use to determine how you are treating yourself. Not to add pressure or guilt, but to put it into a context that is a powerful and relatable reminder.

Over many years of working with clients, I have seen firsthand that we are often not fully aware of how critical we are with ourselves.

The first time I encountered this self-criticism in a client, I was a little shocked at the lack of insight that was displayed. It was very clear to me that this person was very hard on herself. She didn't really like anything about herself and her self-esteem had taken a massive battering from previous 'failed' relationships. She apologised constantly and for a wide range of things—from talking too much to talking too little, crying, not understanding what I meant, not shifting on things quickly enough—you name it, she apologised for it.

You could say that she was unsure and even meek, in a sense. On the inside, toward herself, though, she was a tyrant. There was no apologising there! I would go as far as to describe her internal self-talk as judgmental and ruthless. However, she had absolutely zero awareness of how harshly she treated herself.

I remember the shock on her face when I asked if she thought she was harsh with herself. "No," she said, completely surprised at my suggestion. I'm happy to say that she did eventually come to understand just how destructive her unconscious behaviour was—how much it stopped her from living the life she wanted. Most importantly, she came to understand that she could not have loving relationships with others until she did a complete overhaul of the one she had with herself.

To help you gain some insight into your treatment of yourself, ask yourself these questions:

- How do you feel about your emotions? How do you react to your sadness? Your anger or fear? When you cry, how do you feel about it?

- How do you speak to yourself when you are frightened?

- How you speak to yourself when you don't want to do something? How do you get yourself to do it?

- How do you speak to yourself when you make a mistake or get something wrong?

- What is your inner dialogue when you look at your body? When you are trying clothes on in a changing room?

- Do you ever swear at yourself or call yourself names?

- Do you praise yourself when you do something well?

- Can you list four of your own strengths?

- Are you able to receive compliments without feeling uncomfortable?

Self-awareness can be confronting, but it doesn't have to be negative. By answering these questions, you are just getting an insight into yourself at this moment in time. It's not set in stone. If this exercise has made you feel a little sad, honour that. Sit with it for a while and then know this: the realisation of your inner dialogue when you allow the Inner Critic to be the dominant voice, is something to rejoice. Now that you know, you can choose differently. Only once you see the extent of the effect, can you truly understand the importance of this work.

Just as a child thrives when raised in an environment of love, you thrive when your inner world is supportive, compassionate, and loving. It is misguided to believe that your life doesn't feel good and isn't the way you want it to be because of your childhood. Or because of what someone said to you once. Unless the same thing is happening at this exact moment, it's in the past.

Alternatively, you might think the reason you're unhappy is because of something that's missing. Not having enough money, time or energy. The illness you have. Where you live ... the list is endless. But the real reason you don't feel good is, first and foremost, because you haven't been tending to the 'home' you live in. Your internal world is not supportive. In an unsupportive internal environment, your ego will thrive. Fear, doubt, and judgment will abound, and any access to wisdom, insight, intuition, or relief will seem impossible.

For any relief to come, and for wisdom to be able to reach you, you must shift from fear to love. How do you do that? Well, it's not a one-off thing. There is no magic pill or potion. There is no mantra to repeat or herbal tea to drink three times a day. It is as easy and as difficult as choosing differently every time you are aware.

Firstly, it's important to understand that you have a choice. There is a choice between judging yourself and accepting yourself. There is a choice between hard and gentle. You have this choice about how you perceive yourself. As well as what you do with the input you receive. Will you use it against yourself or *for* yourself? Will you beat yourself up with what you learn about yourself, or will you *build* yourself up with it?

The choice is always yours.

Chapter 7

Set the Tone

*"If you want people to love you, love yourself
and teach them how."*

Guru Singh

So, what exactly do I mean by 'Set the Tone'? To explain the title more than halfway through the book might seem a little late in the proceedings but sometimes you need to clear the path and learn some fundamental things before you get to the heart of the matter. And Setting the Tone *is* the heart of the matter. It's at the core of any transformation that you will achieve. So, what is it and how do you do it?

Setting the Tone is twofold ...

1)   You must create an inner world that is a match to the outer world you want to experience. You must BE what you want to attract.

AND

2)   You must be a living example of what you expect, how you want to be treated, and how you want life to be for you. You have to lead by example.

85

You already know that you can't receive what you are not a match to. If there is no landing place, no matching vibration within you, no amount of praying, affirming, or manifesting technique is going to bring you that experience. Again, this is not because you are not worthy or because some force is actively keeping it from you, this is because you are not BEING what you want.

You cannot receive any of the things you wish to see in your outer world—the loving relationship, the supportive and intimate friendships, the acceptance you wish to feel from your family, the acknowledgment of your contribution from your boss or your clients—unless you ARE these things.

At this point you may be having a reaction to this statement—something along the lines of ... "But I am loving, kind, thoughtful, respectful ... and I'm not seeing it reflected to me in my outside world." So let me say this to you, "How you treat others is *not* the starting place for this work." I am not asking you to be 'nicer' or 'more loving' to others so that they can see how you want to be treated. Sure, the statement "Treat others as you wish to be treated' is always true. But first, "Treat *you* how you want to be treated!" Because your outer world is not a direct manifestation of all the things you wish for—your outer world is, instead, a physical manifestation, or reflection, of your inner world!

You may be wishing for love. You may be affirming it, carrying the word around with you in your pocket as your 'word for the year'—you may even have it emblazoned on your vision board. But if you are not a match to 'love,' because you withhold it from yourself and you focus on your lack of it, then you can't receive it in your outer world. Setting the Tone needs to start with you, and more specifically, your ego.

To BE that which you wish to experience in your life, and to create an inner world in which you thrive, there are three fundamental things you need to learn to do:

- Recognise Ego.
- Separate YOURSELF from Ego.
- Pivot to your Right Mind/Inner Guide.

By now, you know a lot about your ego. And I hope that you are softening toward it because of the information you've received. And you are aware that it spends most of its time overwhelmed. Ego is really an overworked, exhausted, anxious control freak. Although it will fight against handing over power, once you are in charge, it will actually breathe a sigh of relief.

A good way to understand how your ego will respond to YOU taking over, is to watch a few episodes of 'Supernanny.' Do you know this American show with the English nanny, Jo Frost, who arrives in a black cab at the homes of families who need help with their children? When she arrives, the parents, frazzled and at the end of their tether, breathe a sigh of relief that the Super Nanny is there! Yay, she is going to whip these kids into shape and then the family can live happily ever after.

The kids, on the other hand, smell change. And kids don't like change. They also feel a sense of impending doom as they can tell, as soon as Jo enters the house, that she holds a power they have never felt before. Even if it's not a conscious thought,

Set the Tone

there is a knowing in the children that this lady 'Ain't no pushover.' She is not going to crumble like the parents they have spent years wearing down.

The first day always goes something like this ...

The parents feel like Santa has arrived and are beaming with joy. The children, unsure and quiet, are assessing the power of their enemy. They can tell by the way this lady talks to their parents that, 'Shit is about to get real.'

Day two goes something like this ...

Having observed the family dynamic the night before, Jo (aka Super Nanny) has now assessed where the parents are haemorrhaging their power and allowing the children to be in charge. She starts to teach the parents how to handle meltdowns, defiance, power battles, etc.

This is generally the day of tears. Tears from the children, pleading for this lady to go home and for life to return to normal. The kids often look at Jo with absolute hatred and contempt, having concluded that she is ruining their world.

The parents also cry—out of frustration and a sense of failure. This 'Super Nanny' seems to expect *them* to make the changes! She is also saying that somehow, they have had a part to play in the children being the way they are. So, the parents also look at Jo with contempt. After all, they didn't go on this show to be made to look like idiots. Why is this woman not fixing their children?

Day three ...

More tears from everyone. Jo sits the parents down and gives them a stern but loving talking-to that includes words and phrases such as, "Adult," "Lead by example," and "Be in charge."

Day four ...

The light is starting to shine! The children are starting to see the benefits of having boundaries, defined rules with consequences, and they start to feel safer. They become more affectionate, especially with Jo, as they start to realise how good it is that this lady has come and helped their home shift from one of chaos and yelling to one of calm and fun (Jo always encourages family activities and games).

The parents start to realise that Jo doesn't think they are incompetent. And they begin to enjoy spending time with the same children that only a week ago had them pouring themselves a glass of wine by 3pm. They give Jo a big hug goodbye, and there are more tears as they try and figure out if they could get this woman to live permanently in their home until the kids move out.

Super Nanny leaves, but the family continues to be filmed. Then, a week later, just before she returns for one last pep talk and a family hug, she watches the footage. She sees some improvement and some behaviour that went right back to what it was before she arrived. In almost every episode of the show, the children behave in their 'old' way when the parents revert to *their* 'old' way.

This is such an accurate depiction of exactly what happens when you begin to Set the Tone and your ego becomes aware of the 'change' that comes from the shift in power from it to you. Just as the children don't want to lose the control they have established in their home; your ego doesn't want to lose the influence it has established in your mind. And just as the parents want a quick fix from an outside source, so do most people when it comes to changing their lives.

Many people give all their power to others if they think they can help them. They project the energy of, "Tell me what to do, help fix me." But there is no fixing required. Because you are not broken. You do not have a defective mind. You are not weak. What you are most likely doing is handing your power over to an aspect of your mind that, just like the children in my example, doesn't want anything to change. So, please know this: without *you* leading the change, it will never be permanent.

How many times has something inspired you to change? How many times have you read something, heard something, or been to a workshop or seminar and thought, "This is it!" But afterward, you were left to your own devices, and soon enough, you went back to 'business as usual.' Please don't be disheartened by this. No one is at fault here, and neither side has failed.

Sure, some programs aren't designed for you to succeed. After all, you staying a 'customer' is part of the business model. But even with the best of intentions to cause transformation, if it doesn't involve changing your mind it's not permanent. And by permanent, I don't mean 'one time does the trick.' I mean that you gain a self-directed ability to get back on course when you find yourself having fallen asleep on the job.

So how do you learn to recognise the ego and separate yourself from it? The best place to start is by using your feelings as your guide. Here is where many of us hit a snag. As very young children, we are so tuned in to our feelings that, if we are allowed to express them, we do so, release them, and let them go. Nothing gets carried. Every moment is a new moment. Every day is a new day. This is how a toddler can go from having a massive meltdown of epic proportions to sporting a big smile and playing calmly within a very short time. From the perspective of the adult, this can seem like you are watching a psychotic little being!

Unfortunately, rather than being taught to respect our emotions and evolve in terms of how we express them, most of us are taught to not express them at all. We receive messages that we are too loud, too angry, or too joyful. Or, we're told to stop laughing, stop crying, stop singing, stop speaking in that voice. We're told not to ask the lady that question, not to stare at that man, not to say "no" to the food, not to say "yes" to the lolly ...

At every turn we are taught to suppress, ignore, and control our emotions. To control ourselves. No wonder humanity is experiencing addiction, suicide, anxiety, and depression in epidemic proportions. If we don't learn to respect and express our emotions, we can't be fully functioning, healthy human beings.

As we become older and head out into the world, there are even more pressures and rules around 'how to behave appropriately.' I won't list them here, as they could fill an entire book (and I will speak more on them in Chapter 10), but suffice to say that more often than not, women are taught that their emotions make them crazy and men are taught that their emotions make them weak. No one gets out of this programming completely sane. Most of us move into adulthood barely remembering who we actually are.

If I don't remember who I am and how to authentically be me, then how on earth do I even know what I want? This is one of the main reasons why, at heart, most of us don't know what we want our life to be like. We focus on the things we think we should want, what we have been taught will make us happy— money, a relationship, children, a career, things, lots of things. And when they don't bring us the happiness we thought they would, we feel that we have failed or there must be something wrong with us. We question whether we just aren't doing life right.

If you are someone who has yet to find joy in living by society's rules and programs, and if doing what you 'should' is yet to feel right to you, then I say, "Congratulations!" You are ready to be authentically you and to create the life you want—not the one you are supposed to want.

If emotions feel overwhelming or frightening, then I hope it helps to learn that at the core are only two: fear and love. When you remember that how you feel is your greatest navigational system, then you will recognise that without it, you can't choose differently.

You can't recognise that it's ego guiding you if you are too uncomfortable to spend time getting to know your fear. Ego doesn't arrive with a sense of doom. It speaks to you in your own voice (as, of course, does the Inner Guide). Thoughts aren't labelled 'Ego,' so how will you be able to tell whether a thought is from your ego or from you? Mainly, by how the thought makes you feel.

Here are some feelings and other qualities of the experience of a fear (ego)-based thought:

- Tight, narrow, constricted.
- You feel less than/not good enough.
- You are focused on, even obsessed with, detail.
- Focused on the problem. You can't seem to see or feel your way out.
- Overwhelmed.
- You feel inferior or superior.
- You feel alone.
- You feel like an impostor, as if any minute someone, or all of 'them,' will find out you have no idea what you are doing, or that you are incompetent.
- A need to be right and/or the good guy in any situation.
- Feeling like a victim.
- Powerless.
- Feeling or focusing on the separation between us all.
- Catastrophising / focusing on worst-case scenarios.

There are other aspects and feelings that can come into play, but you get the general gist of the most common ones. When you have these feelings and focus on these things, you are not YOU.

You are in ego. To begin the transition to YOU and to return to your power, simply breathe (remember, this begins the 'Power of the Pause') and say, "Ego." You may experience the desire to negate, suppress, or attack limiting or 'negative' thoughts, but these reactions will actively keep you in ego.

I want you to make friends with your fear. I want you to listen to it, respect it, regard it, soothe and comfort it. And then let it know that you are now in charge. Remember me teaching Kassy, 'I've got this'? Well, this is your chance to teach your ego/fear the same thing.

So far, we haven't spoken a lot about the Inner Guide, aka our Right Mind. That's because until you are able to recognise the ego and dial it down, the guide is mostly drowned out. I'm always surprised to see how many courses there are on connecting with your intuition that don't teach participants how to differentiate themselves from their ego/fear. How can you recognise whether a thought like, "He is cheating on you," is coming from your ego or your intuition unless you are familiar with what fear feels like and how it shows up?

Have you ever experienced this: arguing backwards and forwards in your mind; being able to be both prosecution and defence on the same issue? You can get stuck in overwhelm as you go through every possible outcome of a decision and all the pros and cons—and then start again from the start, just in case you missed something. Or you might have a constant stream of 'round and round' thinking like some mental game of tennis where your thoughts are the ball and Fear and your Inner Guide are the players.

Okay, from here on in, know this: It's not two sides that are arguing, debating, presenting their cases, and weighing up the pros and cons. It's the SAME side. It's Ego arguing with itself! You are just the bystander, waiting for your mind to hand you the solution so you can finally act on it. This is all your ego. Your Inner Guide hasn't even gotten a word in yet because your mind hasn't been quiet enough for you to hear it. Also, Love will never argue with anyone or anything. It's not here to convince you.

Your 'job' in all of this is to create the space to connect in with your Right Mind, your Inner Guide. So, what are some practical ways that you can respond when you recognise Ego in your own mind? And how can you consciously use the Power of the Pause to reconnect to your power?

Grab your journal and jot down these prompts for when you recognise an ego thought:

- State 'Ego' or 'Fear' to remind yourself that you are separate from this.

- Say, "It's okay, I've got this. I'll take it from here." This lets your ego know that you are now in charge, you are the adult in the room.

- State, "We are not doing this," when Ego tries to convince you of anything that is other than what you want to be feeling. For example, when it tries to convince you that your friend hasn't texted you back because she doesn't like you, or that you completely messed up the job interview you just had and the interviewers think you are an idiot, and so on and so on. We all know how this goes.

Set the Tone

- Visualise a key in your mind whenever you hear something from your ego and grab it as a symbol of you taking your power back and getting back into the driver's seat of your own life.

- State, "I will not use this against myself," to stop from beating yourself up with your insights, or when you find you're getting judgmental about your reactions or handling of a situation.

These statements, and any others you feel are supportive, will help you move out of fear and into creating your connection with your Inner Guide. How will you know that you are communicating with your Right Mind? How will it feel when you are hearing your Inner Guide?

Here are some feelings and qualities associated with the experience of hearing your Right Mind or Inner Guide:

- Open, calm, expansive.

- There is a focus on solutions and creative ways to solve 'problems.'

- Feeling empowered and inspired.

- Focusing on peace.

- Focusing on your heart's desires.

- You recognise how similar we all are to each other and how connected we are.

- You feel empathy and compassion for yourself, for all people and things.

- You can see the bigger picture regardless of the situation you are in.

- You feel confident and competent.

Set the Tone

- Things seem beyond understanding. Often you don't know how you know what you know, or where the solutions or insight come from.

- You trust in the process of life and feel that everything will work out.

Once you consciously identify and interact with your ego, choose to activate your power, and create a space for guidance from your Right Mind, you are actively moving yourself from fear to love. And now you are ready to consciously Set the Tone.

So, what is it you would like to be feeling within and from the outside world? Love, regard, support, acceptance, joy, being heard ... ? Really think about and feel into this. When you have connected with what you want, write your list down in your journal.

Now, it's time to get to work on making your inner world a match to your list. Let's say you wrote down 'loving' and 'supportive.' You set the tone for this by treating your fear with love and support. And by treating YOU with love and support—through your thoughts, how you speak to yourself, how you respond to what you discover about yourself as you move through life, and how you assess your past or any 'mistakes' you feel you have made.

How does it make you feel to treat yourself how you want to be treated? Does it feel like this is an impossible task and you may as well stop reading and give up now? I am not making light of the fact that this may be a massive shift for you—it certainly was for me. There is nothing easy about this, and there is nothing quick about it. Remember, though, quick and easy are not permanent.

I want you to know that I see you, and I recognise that this can seem overwhelming and beyond your capabilities. You might feel a sense of, "I've tried this before and it never lasts very long." That's because you tried to be more loving with yourself whilst *in* ego. And although I have full faith in your ability to create a loving world for yourself—a space in which you can thrive—I don't have the same faith in your ego. I'm not asking your ego to set the tone; I'm asking *you* to do it!!

You decide what the 'tone' of your inner world is. You decide what is allowed and what is not, what is acceptable and what is not. You encourage love, kindness, compassion, and regard. You allow yourself to be heard and your feelings to be respected. And anytime you experience anything other than this, you recognise that you have moved 'off your path,' 'off track' into fear, and you gently and lovingly redirect yourself back to YOU. To once again setting the tone.

As you become adept at creating an inner world that feels the way you desire, the beauty is that you are BEING exactly what you want to create and receive from the outer world. Your whole life becomes an act of you modelling what you value and what you desire. In this way, you provide an unambiguous and powerful message not only to all of the people around you but to the whole universe.

Chapter 8

When the Critic Becomes a Guide

*"You are the only one in the room whose narrative
you need to pay attention to."*

Matt Kahn.

Imagine you are part of a hypnotist's show. Sitting on a chair on a stage, you are awake and aware of what is happening around you and in charge of your own thoughts and reactions. Then the hypnotist snaps his fingers and says, "Sleep." Your head falls forward, as you have gone into a kind of trance.

If this is anything like the shows I have seen on TV, you are now likely to dance around the stage like a chicken or stand up and play air guitar—whatever the hypnotist has 'programmed' you to do. Then, when he counts you back from ten, snaps his fingers, and says, "You are now awake," you will have no memory of what just occurred.

Throughout much of our lives we are effectively in a trance— 'asleep' to the greatest hypnotist there is (which lives in your mind): The ego. You might be going about your day, feeling good, comfortable, and calm, when you encounter something that sends a jolt through that pleasant state of being. It can be anything—a message or a call, something you see on TV or online—even a memory or a thought. Something 'unpleasant' has just triggered a response. Ego snaps its fingers and says, "Sleep."

The hypnotist is now in charge. And it is annoyed, offended, and ready to go into battle. Unchecked, your ego is always ready for a fight. A friend recently told me about a book she was reading concerning the work of a hostage negotiator. I replied, "We are all hostage negotiators when we are dealing with our ego." Ego comes along, sees an opportunity to take over, and won't 'release' us until its demands are met. It will want maximum drama and a fair amount of conflict. Not to mention a getaway car made up of the regret and fully-admitted responsibility of the person who is the perceived cause of our current discomfort.

So, here are some ways you can maintain a perceived state of peace and ensure you are never triggered:

1). Avoid anything uncomfortable at any cost. Stay at home as much as possible. Avoid relationships, they are a minefield of discomfort. Have no social media accounts and do not watch TV. Avoid spending any time with anyone you don't know or with whom you aren't able to fully control the narrative.

2). Go through your day with all radars on. Ensure your boundaries are firmly in place and be ready to deal with any fucker who thinks you are an easy target to take out of your power. Be clear, be firm on what is and is not acceptable to you. Have a one-strike-and-you-are-out policy. You don't have time for people who treat you with disrespect.

3). Recognise that the discomfort is an opportunity to stay awake and in charge and NOT allow the hypnotist to take over and react on your behalf. Use the opportunity to stay in your power and choose consciously to bring yourself back to peace.

Okay, let's be honest. Numbers one and two are extremes, while to be responding from number three all the time would make you an enlightened being. Most of us are on a spectrum. Sometimes we react consciously, and sometimes we are so deeply asleep it's a wonder we can put one foot in front of the other. But recognising the trigger is what we need to aim for if we desire to stay in our power. Boundaries are one of the key ways to do this, however, most likely not in the way you have come to know them.

The concept of boundaries has been as widely mistaught as The Law of Attraction. Sadly, the misinterpretation of both has left many people believing they are either not doing it right, or they are no good at it. Most mainstream teachings about boundaries can leave you feeling powerless, defeated, or constantly defensive and ready to fight.

Many people understand boundaries as I have described in option 2: there are clear rules and strict consequences for breaking them and crossing the boundary. These boundaries are put in place with the hope of teaching others how to treat you with respect. And so you won't settle for anything less. If this is how you are approaching an empowered life, then I say, "You must be so tired. Sit down and rest."

And now hear this…

What if this is completely misguided? What if this is an ego-construct designed to give you the illusion of having control over other people while keeping you in a perpetual cycle of high alert and disappointment?

What if boundaries are more like this…

There is a space between you and me. We can both move energetically in and out of this space to interact with each other, but it belongs to neither of us. It is a shared territory that no one has complete control over. Our inner space—now that's 100 percent in our control—but the 'space between,' us? To think we have control over that is a delusion.

And this is where the mainstream definition of boundaries falls short and sets us up for feeling like we mustn't be very good at enforcing them. It teaches that we should be able to control what another says or does in relation to us. If we were clear enough, strong enough, or badass enough, we would be able to control this space. At the same time, there is a huge missed opportunity because we put so little focus on our own reactions to what occurs within the shared space.

This results in a constant focus of power outside of us. And a lot of time spent trying to figure out the motives of others. How many times have we given our power away, forgetting that it's only ourselves over which we have any power? How many hours, days, or years, have we spent ruminating over someone's intention at the expense of coming to a deeper understanding of ourselves? All this time and energy keep you from the real work, the real power—the thing that allows for real and lasting change: YOU.

A perfect example of this is how I felt after a conversation with a friend one day, many years ago. The discussion was about my business. Without having been asked, she proceeded to give me her opinions on what I should be doing, along with a whole heap of feedback on what I had already done. Neither of which I had asked for.

While we were on the phone, I was happy with my answers, but I was getting frustrated at even being questioned about my decisions. At this stage of the interaction, I was awake and aware, and I knew that her questions came from a place of having no trust in herself. She was thinking that, if she were me, she would want the feedback.

But by the time I got off the phone, I was annoyed. As the day went on, I felt more and more angry. I'm happy to say that this was not an example of my ego saying, "… And sleep," and then fully taking over while I was still on the phone. It is, however, an example of it playing something over and over, while whispering in my ear, "How dare she?" This happened for long enough that, although I wasn't asleep, I was slowly being taken hostage by the ego, which wanted conflict. It didn't matter that I was no longer on the phone to my friend, or that she wasn't in the room. Ego was happy to take the argument into my imagination.

After a few hours of mental arguing with her, I won the hostage negotiation and the haze started to clear as I became more aware—more me—again. My understanding came in the form of symbolism, as it so often does. My friend's words, her questioning and doubt, put a 'weapon' in the shared 'energetic' territory between us. BUT she did not have the ability to use that 'weapon.' Only I could do that, and I'd been beating myself up with it for hours. I suddenly understood that all those times we have felt as if someone's words or actions are like 'a dagger to the heart' or 'a kick in the guts,' it's been us doing the stabbing and kicking to ourselves.

There really is a genuine boundary where you stop and another person begins. My friend's words and energy could only enter because not only did I give them permission, but I was also the one that brought them into my space! Long after she was off the phone, I still replayed the conversation over and over and kept the whole thing alive. I realised that it's what we do with someone else's words and actions that determine the extent of the damage and the depth of the wounds.

This is what 'having boundaries' really means: I am responsible for what I allow to enter my world.

Having 'good' boundaries means:

I will not use another's words or actions against myself, not even my ego's.

I will not use another's opinion of me against myself, not even my ego's.

I will not use what society tells me about myself, against myself.

I am responsible for my inner world, and I decide what and who comes in.

What will you do with what someone places into that shared space? The choice is yours. You can either handball it to your ego and sleep in the corner while it causes chaos and destruction to your relationships and sense of self, or you can stay awake, breathe, and allow for 'the lesson of the trigger.' What if this space between you and another person, or between you and the outside world, came to be thought of as 'the space of opportunity'?

One of the lessons in *A Course in Miracles* is, "I am never upset for the reason I think I am." This, for me, was life-changing. Long before I genuinely understood it, just repeating it whenever I felt upset allowed for The Pause. When you put this pause in often enough, and learn to lengthen it, you can begin to access a power you never knew you had. When your ego quiets enough for you to start working regularly with yourself and with Right Mind, you can develop a sense of love and compassion that allows any experience to work FOR you. You actively start practising building yourself up.

Triggers are a tricky business. Designed to help you find any unhealed aspects of yourself, they activate your ego like nothing else does. What happens in full trigger mode, full warfare territory, is that someone's ego has triggered yours. This further triggers theirs, which further triggers... well, you get the idea.

Of course, when we encounter someone's ego, we are face to face with their fear, with the least evolved aspect of their mind, that which is focused on survival. What we, ideally, do in the face of fear is respond with love, compassion, and understanding. I saw the most beautiful example of this every time my girl, Kassy, encountered Teddy, a pooch in our neighbourhood.

We first encountered Teddy and his owner, Maureen, one Sunday afternoon. This was before we had our dog, Kassy. We stopped to chat and discovered that Teddy had recently been adopted from the pound. From what Maureen knew of his past, it had been rough.

Over the next few months, we often ran into Maureen and Teddy and we always stopped to chat. The first time we encountered them, after adopting Kassy, the previously shy Teddy responded to Kassy with all guns blazing. He barked nonstop in a tone that left no doubt about how he felt in her presence. Respecting this, we kept our distance, staying across the road and yelling "hello" to each other above the sound of the barking.

Maureen tried everything she could to calm Teddy—all to no avail. He didn't seem aggressive, but he was letting Kassy know that he was not going to have her come any closer—not without permanent damage to her hearing, anyway. This barking went on for the next five years, every time we saw them. It did decrease in severity and extent, such that we were eventually able to stand on the same side of the road.

And here is what I found so impressive about the whole scenario: Kassy never reacted to Teddy's barking—not once. In fact, she usually seemed happy to see him! Each time we came across the pair on our walks, she would get a little spring in her step, wag her tail in excitement, and then sit and be barked at until he calmed down. I found this extraordinary.

One day, after watching her not react for the umpteenth time, I realised that Kassy understood that he was frightened and that it had nothing to do with her. She totally understood that his reaction was not personal. While he was being triggered, most likely due to his past experiences, she was just peacefully staying centred and in her power.

Now here was an example of boundaries like I'd never seen before. She knew they weren't ever going to be friends, but she could also encounter him without giving her power away. This show of compassion and regard for someone else's feelings without making it be about her will stay with me for the remainder of my days as an example of a master level of 'setting the tone.'

Our lessons are not learnt by ensuring we are never triggered but by asking, "Why did that trigger me?" That's where our gold is. When we can consciously stay with our reaction—stay awake in the face of pain and discomfort—we find that the Critic has become the Guide. Triggers highlight what needs attention, which beliefs have been activated, and what we can shift perspective on. They show us where we are forgetting our power and forgetting who we are.

Let's find some of your own gold. Grab your journal.

I want you to have a think about who has had, or still has, a large negative effect in your life. Whether or not they are still in your life doesn't matter. How long ago they had the impact also doesn't matter. Write down the names of anyone you can think of who has had a 'negative' effect in the way they made you feel, spoke to you, or treated you. Leave a few lines between each one.

Then, write a couple of sentences describing how they had a negative impact on you. What did they do? How did they make you feel? What negative or limiting beliefs did they set up in you? Spend as much time on this as you like. If a few lines are not enough, then continue onto another page. Write it all out until it feels like you are done.

*** Do this without reading ahead.

Once you have completed this, turn to a new page and again write their names down, leaving some space between each one. Now write the heading "My Teachers" at the top of the page. This time, I would like you to spend a few minutes connecting with the opportunity that this person has provided to you. What did their words and/or behaviour help teach you that benefits you?

For example, they might have taught you to walk away from an unhealthy relationship, or maybe they taught you how competent you are, how independent you can be, or how strong and capable you are. Maybe they were the person who finally taught you to say, "no"? Maybe they were someone who taught you where your line is, and to recognise what is not acceptable for you. Maybe they gave you the opportunity to choose you, to recognise what you want—by showing you a whole lot of what you don't want?

This is not an exercise in forgiveness. Even if you still experience anger, sadness, or any other unresolved feelings, you can look for the lesson that is here for you. You can even take the person out of it, take all the details away, cross out the person's name, and ask, "What did I learn from this experience that serves me well?"

Now, this can get your ego alert and ready to take over with thoughts like, "I'll let you know what they taught me, they taught me not to trust anyone, not to be an idiot, not to be fooled and believe what people say . . ." Hmm, does that sound like information that builds you up or beats you up? Ego will use anything it can against you, hoping that it will stop you from being 'weak' and 'vulnerable' again in the future. Your Inner Guide, in contrast, wants you to build yourself up with anything you experience, and use what you learn as you navigate life to reach ever-greater levels of trust, compassion, and love for yourself and others.

Take some time to read over your list, genuinely connect in with your heart and ask, "What did I learn about myself that serves me well? That builds me up?"

It is at this point that I have a ground-breaking truth to share with you. Are you ready? I hope you are sitting down.

Okay, here goes: your life is about YOU.

I know, it's a shock, isn't it? Who knew? Here we were, thinking that it's about our parents, and then our friends, and then our partners, and kids, and our jobs and our homes, and our money, and...

But all this time it was simply and purely about us. No one else—just us. And everything we thought it was about (and tried to control, change, and manipulate into what was better or best), was really always perfect, just as it was. The reason for this perfection? Because the only thing it was designed for was to teach us about ourselves and guide us to renavigate if we ventured off course.

Every trigger is a sign that we are off course. If we are taken hostage by our ego, asleep in the chair and waiting to react from an old program, we are off course. If we meet fear, our own or someone else's, with more fear (and judgment and criticism), we are off course. If we are waiting on someone or something else to change before we can have the experience we want to, we are off course. If we are trying to teach others how to treat us without treating ourselves that way, we are off course. If we think we can experience anything outside of us that we don't already have on the inside, we are off course. If we believe we are in any way not enough, broken, damaged, or defective, we are off course.

What is the 'course?' The 'course' is a journey through life whilst being connected to Source and your Inner Guide in an ever deeper and more expansive expression of all that you are. Your work is to remove all that keeps you from that.

Although it might appear as if certain people, experiences, or things can keep you from being 'on course,' the only thing that can ever really do that, is you. All the work worth doing occurs on the inside since, as I remind you once again, the outside is only a reflection of the inside.

The trigger is a sign that we have some healing to do. The person or thing that triggers us is no more responsible than the doctor who presses on an ankle that was twisted during a fall. The doctor helps you find the injury but he or she didn't create the wound. So, is all this saying that no one ever needs to take ownership for what they say or do to you, and that there should be no consequences? No, of course not. But knowing that a trigger is about you, and taking full responsibility for your reaction to it, allows for a pause. This, in turn, gives you the opportunity to stay awake and respond from your Right Mind, from your compassionate and loving self rather than from your ego. This means that you stay in your power and don't react or make decisions from a place of fear or from past conditioning.

The outcome might be the same. For example, someone treating you with disrespect may be the end of the relationship either way, but when you make this decision from your ego, without your trigger resolved, you just make the wound bigger for next time. You build in resentment. You most likely carry all the emotions and 'damage' around with you, even though you have physically removed the person from your life. If you are still using what they did or said against yourself, they may as well still be in your life!

Deciding to end a relationship or friendship from your Right Mind, from a compassionate and loving perspective, is not necessarily without pain. It comes from a place of love—love for yourself as you realise at this time, this person is, not who you wish to have a relationship with. And love for the other person as you give up the desire to have them be anything other than they are.

Pausing to allow for guidance does not make you weak. Stopping to reflect on your part in something and why you are reacting the way you are does not make you a pushover. In fact, quite the opposite is true. When you meet yourself and others with compassion and understanding, knowing that we can all be lost in Ego at times, and not sleepwalking through a trigger, you allow for change. You set a tone that is powerful. You allow for pain to be a guide—in your own life and in your relationships.

When you can do this, you model how to be more aware and alert to triggers. When someone knows that being human doesn't denigrate them in your eyes, they will be kinder and more loving with their own pain, more willing to talk about it, more willing to stay awake.

I always say that a healthy relationship is one in which only one person is crazy at any particular point in time. If both people are crazy at the same time, it's explosive, and if both people are crazy all the time, it's toxic. But focusing on 'fixing' them will never change your experience in the relationship.

The change begins with you—from the inside out.

Looking at your 'mental filing cabinet' journal work from Chapter Five; you have valuable information about your triggers. If you grew up not being heard, when you now feel someone isn't listening to you, it will trigger you. This is true even if this person is doing this for the first time in your relationship; even if they *are* listening but you don't *feel* heard. That's the thing with a trigger, it's really a wound from the past that's activated in the present by an unsuspecting person. And this catalyst sends you into a reaction just like it did when the wound was first established.

Ask yourself, "What are my triggers?" What gets me extra fired up? Extra hurt? Can you see the origins in the journal in front of you? On a separate page, write down any triggers that you identify. Head the page with the title "My Triggers – My Freedom." Jot down any triggers that you can think of or that come to you as you look over your work from Chapter Five. Maybe it's rejection, not being heard, being ignored, being spoken over, being told what to do, being treated like a child . . . maybe it's all of these, or something entirely different. You can come back to this section any time you think of more. Life will certainly give you the opportunity to experience them!

Start to be aware of when your blood boils, you get so upset that tears instantly spring to your eyes, you reject something outright, or you want to throw your hands up in the air and say, "I give up." Listen to what the inner critic says. Be aware. Stay with the pain. And ask yourself, "What am I really upset about? Does this remind me of something from my childhood?" Allow for the pause, allow for the lens of your perception to shift beyond merely seeing more and more evidence of the past.

One of my clients was triggered by her ex-husband every time their son went between their two homes. Through all the work she had done, she was able to stay in her power most of the time. Except when he was standing right in front of her. She felt that he could, if he wanted to, make her life hell.

Based on his past behaviour, she had good reason to be worried. Her ex-husband was very aware of how to use his 'power' to intimidate. But if she was going to continue to use the past to determine the present, how could anything change? And if he could keep pulling her out of her power, taking her off course, then how could she ever have freedom from him? In one of our sessions together, I took her through a guided meditation.

I asked her to imagine the scene in *The Wizard of Oz* in which Dorothy and the other characters finally come across the Wizard. Do you remember his booming voice, loud sounds, and ability to instil fear in everyone who came across him? In the movie, Dorothy senses that something is not quite right and looks 'behind the curtain' to find a small man merely operating a machine that allows him to sound larger than he is. This 'cover up' conceals his insecurities and feelings of powerlessness. I talked my client through this scene, and when she looked behind the machine, I asked her to see her ex-husband as the man behind the curtain.

I didn't do this to make fun of her ex-husband or to belittle him, but rather to get her to understand that real power is never used to control or manipulate another person. When someone does that, it is because they are the ones that feel small and frightened. They need all the extra noise and the proverbial 'light show' to make them seem bigger and more powerful than they feel. I wanted her to understand that her ex-husband only had as much power over her as she was willing to give him.

This was several years ago now, but recently she mentioned to me how much of a turning point this was for her. It allowed her to completely shift how she saw him, and she stopped being frightened of what he could do to her. None of this would have worked if she hadn't been willing to take responsibility for changing her mind, allowing herself to see him in a different light, and investigating what he was triggering for her every time she saw him.

With all of this in mind—with all of the knowledge that you now carry about what changing your mind can do for you, and the recognition that nothing can change until you do—let's now take a step into creating the life that you do want to be experiencing.

Let's create consciously!

Chapter 9

Creating New Outcomes

*"A mind which is not crippled by memory
has real freedom".*

J. Krishnamurti

Do you know what you want? If a fairy godmother or a genie popped up in your room right now and said, "I will grant you three wishes," would you know what you wanted? How long would it take you to answer? Are your desires material? Are they experiences? Are they emotions?

The granting of wishes is always a complex scenario. Do you wish for one luxury thing, and then add in good health and world peace? Or do you cleverly come up with a way where one of your wishes leads to an ongoing stream of gifts? Is this a reality we can experience? Can we tap into a stream that allows us to create all that we desire?

Imagine this…

You are a young child and your mum needs something from the supermarket. Just one thing. You ask, 'Can I go and get it? PLEASE!' And you are over the moon with excitement when, for the first time ever, you can go to the supermarket all on your own. She tells you what she needs and puts the money in your coat pocket. You set off, excitedly repeating over and over in your mind what you need to buy. When you get to the supermarket, everything looks so big! You have never been here on your own before, and so everything seems a little different and a little daunting.

You start to head down the aisles looking for what you are meant to buy, and you find yourself in the lolly aisle. Oh Lordy! The smells! The colours! Row after row of deliciousness starts to take over your mind and hijack your attention. The longer you smell the sugar and imagine how good all of this would be to eat, the more you forget what you came to the shop for. After a while, you cannot contain yourself and you start eating some of the sweets.

In the back of your mind, you occasionally have a feeling (and even a worry) that you are here for something specific, and you have forgotten what it is. The longer you spend in the aisle, the more confused you get, to the point you even forget that you have a home or a mother waiting there for you. You become so obsessed, so driven figuring out what you can get and how you can eat all of these sweets that you literally forget yourself. You forget who you are and what you came here for.

You wander aimlessly up and down the aisle, occasionally eating, occasionally discovering something you hadn't seen before. But the more time you spend here, the more unhappy you feel. You sense there is something missing, but you don't know what it is. When other people enter the aisle, you ask them, "Excuse me, do you know what I came here for?" Sometimes they give you suggestions, and sometimes they say they are certain they know what you came for. But none of their answers feel right to you.

Also, ironically, the longer you spend in the lolly aisle, the less sweet it all tastes. The less excited you feel about all the colours and the flavours. And the stronger the feeling gets that there is something that you are here to do. Still, you just can't seem to remember what.

Can you relate to the feeling that something is missing? Do you have a yearning for something but don't know what? I would hazard a guess and say that every human on the planet feels a sense that something is 'missing' at some point in time. If we give this 'problem' to our ego to solve for us, then it will be like the child caught in the lolly aisle. Ego will assume that what is missing is what it has observed and been taught to value whilst growing up in your family, and also by wider society and culture. (More on this in Chapter 10.)

Ego will come to conclusions like:

- There is a sense of 'missing' because I am not loved enough.

- There is a sense of 'missing' because I have not met 'The One.'

- There is a sense of 'missing' because I don't have enough money.

- I don't have the right house, car, clothes, shoes, job, hair, thighs, body, intelligence, friends, partner to fill the 'missing' and the 'yearning.'

Ego will encourage you to do what it always does, which is 'look on the outside for the right 'thing' or person to fill the hole. To fill that feeling of incompleteness. And just like the child in the supermarket, we can get caught in a never-ending trap of 'things,' believing they will make us feel better.

So, when we are actively focusing on change in our lives, how do we get to know what we want? Well, by now you have your 'mental filing cabinet' accessible to you and you are beginning to see the basis of patterns and triggers. You require two things to shift into purposeful creation from the subconscious programs that you now recognise. You need to move beyond your ego, and get clear on what you want to draw to yourself instead.

Why bypass the ego? Because it thinks it's a fortune teller. However, it doesn't have the power to tell your future—it only has the ability to tell you your past, and then convince you that your future will be the same. If you allow Ego to do the creating, the decision making and the visioning, you won't be able to move beyond perceptions of the past to consciously create new outcomes.

Have you ever heard of the saying, "the devil's in the details"? Well, you know what? So is your ego. This is why, when I first learned the concept of highly specific and measurable goals in my Kinesiology training, something felt off. This way of setting goals seemed perfect for making a plan with my builder on the renovations of my house, with wanting to learn a new skill, or with my PT as I trained for a marathon. But to use it to create a great life just felt limited. Let me share with you why.

The more specific I get, the more excited my ego gets. Because specificity appeals to its control-freak nature. Ego can decide exactly what, when, where, and who—all the details—down to a tee. It seems to me that when I am doing this, I can only use what I already know to create more of the same limited outcomes. The more detailed I get, the more I am drawing from the past and my own limited understanding of how life will show up for what is possible. There's no creativity here. There's no space or opportunity for God (Spirit, the Universe, Source, Universal Wisdom, Aunty Betty) to come in and create perfection.

Oooohhhh, here's a relevant tangent. How does the word 'perfection' make you feel? I have often had clients display a real rejection of that word. They describe themselves as recovering perfectionists and do not even want the word to be mentioned in our sessions, let alone in any affirmations they might work with. I get it. When perceived through the lens of an ego, perfection is an unattainable outcome—an impossible achievement designed to keep us all feeling 'not enough.'

However, there is another way to view perfection. Through the lens of our Right Mind, our Inner Guide, and Love, perfection becomes something that is created *through* us, not *by* us. Our perfection is a given—we are each perfect as we are. We don't need to create perfection, because it's already there, in everything. We can, however, get in the way of it. If the word 'perfection' is not something that you feel you can work with at this point, then simply substitute the word 'flow.'

Let me take you back to the supermarket and the lolly aisle for a few minutes. Remember the note our mum slipped into our coat pocket, the one with what we had to remember on it? Well, each one of us has a 'note' in our pocket from our 'between lives' meeting with the panel and set designers, which occurred before we stepped into this life.

At the top of the paper is written, "Soul Expansion and Evolution." This is the same for each one of us. Underneath this is written a unique purpose and our individual lessons. It might be freedom, remembering my power, finding my voice, choosing myself, acceptance… these are different for each of us.

At this very moment in time many of us are sitting in the 'lolly aisle' surrounded by wrappers, feeling sick to the stomach with how full we are and yet, feeling so empty. This is what an ego creation looks and feels like. There's a lot of wrappers, and a lot of stuff, but a big pit of emptiness.

If this is you, or if you can relate to the 'something missing' feeling, take a deep breath. As you breathe in, feel love and wisdom enter every part of your body, heart and mind.

Now, close your eyes and see yourself putting your hand in your pocket. See yourself taking out the note that is there and handing it to your Right Mind, your Inner Guide. Take another deep breath as you feel relief washing over your whole being. See Right Mind take the note and hear your guide say, "Let's do this together."

The unfolding of perfection in our lives can be defined in our experience of the perfect set of circumstances—selected specifically for our evolution. In order for this to happen, it is vital we understand that from our current vantage point, we are not able to fully connect with the bigger picture perspective, nor with all of the information that ultimately allows our life to make 'sense.' And therefore, I remind you to trust the set designers.

Let me share an example of allowing perfection to unfold. This was a perfection that I could only have gotten in the way of, had I been allowed (or able) to control the details.

A few years ago, Mr Cookson and I moved into the house in which we currently live. It is, indeed, perfect in ways we couldn't have possibly planned. When we began the house-hunting process, this was what we knew for sure: we wanted green, we didn't want it to feel like a 'normal' suburban house, we knew it could not be further than a certain distance from Mr Cookson's work, and my own personal stipulation was that it be close enough to some nature trails that I could easily go on local hikes. For example, being near a local mountain range would totally fit the bill.

From the hiking I had already done, I was reasonably familiar with one side of the mountain range. I liked it, so I figured the next task was to pick a particular town or area on that side of the mountains. This is where my 'past' started to cloud my present choices. I had my heart set on the places I knew and loved, but we quickly realised that our budget wasn't going to get us very much in those areas. To be crystal clear in our understanding of this process, at the time, my focus was on two things: what we could afford and a few very specific geographic areas.

Every now and again, a house I loved the look of would come up in an area I knew I definitely didn't want to live in. But as I faced the 'reality' of our budget, I was starting to become a little more willing to expand my geographic boundary. We had been advised to sell our house before buying a new one so as not to create any pressure or desperation to sell for possibly much lower than we wanted to. So, we started to get our house ready for sale and we kept a constant eye on the real estate app we were using to track the local market. Mr Cookson and I would both spend every spare minute looking at the app and, in the end, all the houses started to seem like a mishmash of each other. Which was the one with the great garden? Did you see the one with the renovated kitchen? Are you willing to live here? Should we up our budget by $50,000?

All of these thoughts and actions came from a place of limitation—a stance of, "This is how much money we have, and this is what we can get for it. We don't 'love' any of these places and we are starting to look at areas we said we would never live in BUT we will have to face reality and just pick the one that is most like what we are looking for." What a way to create out of limitation!

One day, we expanded our search. Somehow, a house from the 'other' side of the mountain snuck into the mix. This house was in a town that neither of us knew or had ever been to before. We decided to check it out. By this time, we had decided to proceed with the sale of our house despite the conventional wisdom. So, as the set designers would have it, we arrived at the open house on the 'other' side of the mountain on a massive high, having just sold our house at auction two hours prior. However, my first impression was that this house was not at all what I had imagined when I had visualised our life in the hills. Now, at this point, if I had been really stuck on the details, when we walked in I would have said, "It's a nice house but far too small," and then walked right back out. Having swiftly concluded that this was not our home.

But fortunately, I didn't do that. Because once we walked from the front door through the lounge and into the dining room and saw the view from the deck, not to mention the garden, we were in love. If you had asked me at that stage, "How do you like the house?" I would have said, "What house"? The house had completely left my mind as we headed out into the garden and into what I can only describe as a magical place that blew my mind.

As I took in the two majestic oaks in the drive, the giant pines, the literally hundreds of trees that were everywhere I looked, I ended up in the bottom of the garden and heard running water. I was standing in what could be our garden, listening to running water! And I was looking at a walking track that was, quite literally, *next to* the property.

As I stood looking around me and listening to the running stream, I said aloud, "Can people live like this?" I didn't know that you could have walking tracks, running water, gardens that felt like parks, and birdlife, like you lived in a sanctuary—for *our* budget! The house and everything about it was a complete surprise to both of us, and they were—and are—absolutely perfect.

How did I 'manifest' a home that I didn't even know could exist? The simple answer is actually that I didn't. I didn't manifest it. I got out of the way and I allowed it. I didn't vision board it. I didn't sit for hours and imagine my perfect house. I didn't write down a specific goal. I didn't even write an affirmation. I shot a great desire into the Universe, and then I focused on the priorities with as little detail as possible: green, hiking, one hour to work.

Then I trusted and allowed perfection to unfold. Of course, you could argue that the house isn't perfect, but it really has been absolutely perfect in hindsight. About a year and a half after moving in, I became very unwell, and I cannot tell you how many times I have thanked God that the house isn't any larger than it is.

This is not the only time this kind of thing has happened. I have experienced it in all areas of my life. As I allow my life to unfold—as I move through life with open hands and a big heap of trust, it just gets better and better. It's not that there are no challenges. It's just that even the challenges are perfect in terms of the opportunities they bring, as they allow me to grow more and more genuinely into my power.

At this point, you might be thinking, "I want to know what is written on my piece of paper!" Delving into this is beyond the scope of this book, in fact it could most likely fill a whole other book. But here is the good news – you don't need to know what your note says to start creating consciously. And the more consciously you create, the clearer the answer will become for you.

When I felt at my most 'empty' and when the desire for change was at its highest, I had no idea what I wanted. If came across a genie lamp and was given the option of three wishes, I probably would have wished to 'feel better' three times!! I knew what I wanted to move away from, but I didn't know what I wanted to move towards. I knew what I wanted less of, but I didn't know what I wanted to take its place. One of the things that had me feeling so stuck was that I thought I needed to know what I wanted. Ironically the not knowing was the perfect place to create change from.

So, when you let go of the details, what do you focus on instead? You get clear on your values and priorities, and you make choices based on these. I knew that I wanted to leave nursing for nineteen years, but I had no idea what to do instead. This 'not knowing' kept me from making choices that could have brought me clarity a lot earlier.

Just like the focus on 'green, hiking, one hour commute' led me to the perfect house. The focus on 'freedom, no structure, fully myself' has enabled me to invest in the career I now have. This is not a one-step process. But when you are clear on what you want then there is an ease to your decision making that enables you to stay in the moment, connected to your power, like never before.

Creating consciously requires making choices that bring you more of what you want and less of what you don't want. With each choice, you move closer to your desired outcome.

Grab your journal now and have a think about what your values and priorities are. Feel into what you want to move toward.

Write down as many things as come to mind or heart.

Freedom? Family? Abundance? Spaciousness? Self-respect? Health? Empowerment? Love? Peace? Creativity. More time for _____ (reading, cooking, friends, quiet, art, dance?)

Pick one or two that feel the most appealing to you. (Starting with one might be the easiest until you become more comfortable and familiar with this process.)

Write down your priority but no other information. We don't need details. We don't need the why, the what, or the how. Bringing in these kinds of questions will only move this whole exercise over to your ego. Once you bring in details, you bring in guilt and the need to justify.

Once you have chosen the value or priority to focus on, write it down and circle it. This is now what all decisions and choices will be measured against.

Let me share an example with you -

Over the past few years, I have been experiencing some health issues. As you can imagine, this puts health high on my list. If I were to do this exercise right now, I would have the word 'health' written on the page of my journal with a big circle around it.

When I am faced with any decision or choice, I ask myself, "Does this benefit my health or not?" So, when I am tired and a friend asks to meet me, I ask myself, "Will this be of benefit to my health, or will it be detrimental?' This takes all the guilt, all the 'shoulds' and 'have-to's,' out of the decision making and puts the power back in my hands. If I proclaim that my health is a priority for me, then I make decisions that bring me 'more' good health and not 'less' good health.

This priority is not just about how you spend your time, it's about when and how you work, where you live, what you eat, and so on.

Are you able to recognise that the details become secondary when you are clear on the core priority? Any decision making becomes a conscious and clear process that bypasses the ego and its rules and fears of being judged.

Here is another example - Let's say your priority is 'empowerment.'

As you make decisions and are faced with choices throughout your day, week and month, you ask yourself, "Does this make me feel more in my power or less?"

With your values and priorities as your focus, you also set the tone for what is important to you. "Don't bother asking Jenny out on a Thursday night; that's her family night." Or, "Don't bother ringing Karen on a Tuesday; that's her day for herself. She won't answer the phone." This is very powerful. And not personal at all! There is no need for feelings of guilt or rejection. This technique ends the feelings of resentment that accompany you when you say "yes" to things that go against your priorities.

When the focus you have chosen no longer feels right, or when you are receiving plenty of what you want, move onto a different value. Keep going with the flow of your needs and desires. Keep choosing you!

The more you can do this process as a regular part of your day, the more consciously you will be creating the life you want to live. So far, you have created space, cleared out old programs, and learnt the importance of setting the tone. Now it's time to experience that shift in the outer world, as part of the collective.

Chapter 10

A Whole New World

"If you want to awaken all of humanity then awaken all of yourself...
Truly, the greatest gift you have to give is that of your own self transformation".

Lao Tzu

If I were to walk by your side, holding your hand and guiding you through your life journey, I would whisper to you constantly, "Focus within. This where your work lies, this is where the answers are." With this advice, I would be helping you to connect deeply to your purpose and individual evolution. But we are not here only for that purpose.

We are also here at this time, on this planet, with a collective purpose—that of evolving the whole of humanity. There are many wonderful books and teachers that speak on this topic from a wide variety of perspectives, so we won't delve into this here. My intention is simply to bring your awareness to this truth, and to bring the concepts of ego and Right Mind, and shifting from fear to love, into the realm of the collective.

It appears to us as if we were all separate beings having individual experiences. And to a certain extent, we are. Our experience is unique, different from one another's because our filters (and therefore our perceptions, beliefs, and biases) are different from one another's.

A part of stepping up and rising into our full power also involves taking responsibility for, and being conscious of, what we bring to the collective. It's time to learn that just as the environment has a powerful effect on us, we have a powerful effect on it. Awareness of this symbiotic relationship is the key to playing our part in the evolution of the whole.

Imagine this…

Every day we are invited to a big extended family feast. Each evening we all share the main meal, which is a massive pot of soup. The soup stock is the same every day. But the other ingredients are always different, as each one of us brings something to add to the pot. We each pick our ingredient in the morning and then carry it with us all day long. Here, it marinates in the energy that we feel and express throughout our day. By late afternoon, we all arrive at the gathering place and put our ingredients into the pot.

As the ingredients simmer in the stock, we sit for hours and share our day with each other. Then, at a certain time each evening, we all line up and grab a big bowl of that day's soup. We sit around the fire and consume everyone's contribution to the meal. Then, we go to sleep and do it all again the next day.

I want the symbolism of this story to seep into your very being. I want each one of us to be aware that there is a collective pot of energy which we are all attached to. This energy flows all around us, between us, and through us. Not only do we receive from this collective pot, but we are also constantly adding our contributions to it. Just like with the family feast, everything we add has been marinating in our energy and intentions, and every bowl of soup we consume contains the whole group's energy.

You could think of this collective pot like a collective mind, and therefore recognise that just as we each have an ego and a Right Mind, there is also a collective ego (Fear) and a collective Right Mind (Love). The work required of you to help the collective is no different to what brings relief and freedom in your own mind.

This sense of collective is already taught to us, but in a manner that is *by* the ego and *for* the ego. Here's what I mean: "What are you adding to the collective pot?" is a question that is often put to us, through the words, "How are you contributing to society and what is your value as a member of the group?"

In a Western culture, these questions are really referring to productivity and wealth. And yet, we get taught zero to very little about our power to contribute to the energetic frequency of the collective. Or about how to be a healthy member of society. I have a vision for a society that asks its members, "Are you adding to the fear (feeding the ego) or the love (feeding the Right Mind) on the planet?"

One look at the predominant messaging of the Mainstream Media (MSM) at this time, and it's quite easy to see that we are encouraged to be frightened. We are also encouraged to look outside of ourselves for information and guidance on all things. But most especially on our bodies and our health.

At the time of this writing, we live in a period where regular live coverage from our politicians lets us know what we can and cannot do, who we can and cannot see, and even how far we can travel from our homes. Each of our individual responses to this will depend on our particular programming about authority figures, rules, and even intelligence and intuition. All of these will factor into whether you feel you have choices and access to your own power. It will also determine how comfortable or uncomfortable you feel about being told what to do—or told to go against what your instincts tell you.

What a 'perfect' time this would be to completely go back to forgetting our power, and to wait for the outside world to be different before we can 'get on with it'. Before we can be on purpose again. Doing our inner work and learning to thrive in any environment. Alternatively, what an opportunity to recognise that regardless of the outside, *we* set the tone.

This is not to make light of the loss, grief, and fear that so many humans have experienced and are still living through. It does, however, remind us to go within for our anchors, our stability, and our answers.

I'm not suggesting that there is no wisdom to be found in our world—in fact it is all around us. But our collective evolution will come to fruition when we become aware of the ego in the outer world as much as we are aware of it in the inner world. And when we choose Love/Right Mind instead of Fear, we benefit this expansion. So how do we recognise when we are encountering Ego? Well, just like in our internal world, the biggest clue will be in how the messaging makes us feel.

When I was about five years old, I had an extraordinary experience in church. For as far back as I can remember, I have had a sense of God. My parents were atheists, but my nanna was a regular churchgoer, so maybe I got my sense of God from her. Actually, it's not possible to grow up in Austria and not have a sense of God. The local church bell struck every day at 12 p.m., and back in the seventies when I was in kindergarten, the nuns still taught in the local government school. The local priest was the Religious Instructions teacher at school, and the whole class participated in their First Communion as a group. So, there was really no way not to have a sense of God and church, regardless of the messaging at home.

Almost every Sunday, I went to church with my nanna. One of my earliest memories is of one such Sunday, when I heard a clear guidance. Sitting in the pew of the nearly 800-year-old building, I was doing what I normally did in church. I breathed in the frankincense burning in the giant incense lanterns. I stared at the huge, coloured glass windows directly behind the priest. And then glanced with great admiration at the nuns who took up the first pew.

Suddenly, whilst being lost in my own thoughts, I heard a very clear voice say, "Don't listen to anything that is said here." I had never experienced anything like this before, and yet, I didn't feel any fear. The voice left as suddenly as it arrived, and I remember feeling totally calm about the whole experience.

At the time, I didn't put a name to that voice. I didn't feel the need to. Even at age five, I knew it was a loving guidance. It was a directive I listened to wholeheartedly, and it had a profound and lasting effect on my relationship with God. What that experience allowed me to do was to have my own relationship with God: just God and I—no interference.

I've often thought of the power this gift gave me, as I've come across many people from all religions who were scarred by their experience of God—due to a middleman, and the church in general. Many people have been left feeling 'less than,' rejected, dirty, shamed, and like they are 'sinners.' Eventually, some feel that the only way forward is to either reject themselves, or the very concept of God as a whole.

For me, this was never the case. Thank God! (Pun intended.) Because of that one powerful piece of guiding advice—"Don't listen to anything that gets said here"—I never took on anything that I didn't first run by my own 'gut', to feel into whether it resonated with me. The God I knew was loving, kind, accepting, and encouraging. None of the teachings of sin, vengefulness, Hell, and so on ever resonated with me. They just didn't feel right. I intuitively knew not to go outside myself to get a sense of God. I did not need a middleman to connect me with wisdom.

I was not as fortunate when it came to my sense of self and body image. The first time my weight was commented on, I was about six-years-old. I was always tall for my age and looked much older than I was. I had always been fairly slim and had a normal weight, but at around this age, although my arms and legs stayed slim, I developed a bit of a belly. I remember hearing an extended family member mentioning my weight gain to my mum, and that she should watch out that I didn't keep putting weight on. I also grew up with my mum and closest female relatives often talking about their own bodies and their desire to lose weight.

This, along with the media messaging of, 'thin is beautiful,' created the perfect storm of programming. This agenda led to a hatred of my body, a disordered perception of my size, and an unhealthy relationship with food. These two examples of God/religion and body image may seem to be worlds apart, but there are far more similarities in the messaging than you might think. I was spared the toxic church teachings of, "You as a human are inherently flawed and less than," but the media got to me, since I was (understandably) asleep to the toxic messaging showing up in another way.

Fear can be found anywhere, in any walk of life, in any organisation, in any message. When we encounter the messaging, "You are not enough," we must instantly become awake and alert, and activate a remembrance of who we are. Otherwise, we are powerless victims to whomever triggers our fears and doubts. This leaves us open to being manipulated and to acting against ourselves.

We are taught early on to go against ourselves. Children are told to kiss adults they don't want to, or to hug the relative they barely know (and may well get a creepy feeling from.) Girls are taught to be 'nice' and boys are taught to be 'brave.' There is, of course, nothing wrong with being encouraged to be kind or courageous, but there is something very off with this being a regular message, regardless of the circumstance.

The 'not enough' messaging ramps up when we start to be exposed to the media. We have billion-dollar industries that rely on our 'not enoughness.' The advertising industry is a great place to begin to become aware of how much this messaging purposefully speaks to your ego. You know how some ads are very specifically aimed at your children, even though they are obviously not the ones making the purchase? The advertisers know that you want to give your children what they desire—in the same way advertisements are speaking directly to your ego to trigger desires for things you may not even really want!

Have you ever experienced this? I remember when iPhones first came on the market. I paid no attention to them as I was happy with my phone. After a few years, the advertising messaging got to me. And I clearly remember the day I thought, "they've finally done it. I actually want one now!"

So, from birth onward, the messaging from one source or another is, "You are not enough," and we are systematically groomed into being consumers of products that will make us "better." Even if you think you are aware of this, it still has a powerful effect on your subconscious and can come out in ways you are not aware of. In subtle and not so subtle ways, we have all been programmed to believe things that are not necessarily true. We've been taught that men are better than women. White people are more beautiful, intelligent, and trustworthy than brown or black people. Muslims are more violent than any other religion. Thin is more beautiful. Younger is more desirable and attractive than older. Older is wiser than younger. And on and on and on.

None of these assumptions or biases are based on actual truth. However, they are ingrained in us to the extent that we were programmed with what we saw when we were children. These are universal beliefs that we all must become aware of, and challenge, in order for change to occur.

In the same way that the person questioning the status quo of a family is the black sheep, the person questioning what they are taught at school is a troublemaker. And the person questioning long-held societal assumptions can become an outcast. The collective ego is exactly the same as the ego in your own mind. It doesn't like change. It wants to stay in control because that works for it, and it doesn't want to enter some great unknown.

In order for the collective ego to stay in control, the messaging that, "You are not enough," is very well-planned and thought-out. Staying asleep to this aspect of your external experience keeps you a perpetual consumer, victim, and prisoner to both your own ego and that of the collective.

Being able to identify this lower, collective aspect and separate yourself from it, and then choose differently is as freeing for you as a member of the collective, as it is in your own mind as an individual. As the collective ego creates scenarios and industries based on our feeling of not being enough. It triggers our own ego into staying active and in charge in our own minds. But just as we can shift from fear to love, and turn the critic into a guide in our inner world, we can also do this consciously in our outer world. Each time we do so, we defuse the power of the collective ego and we raise the vibration of the 'collective pot.'

Recognising Ego and Fear in the outer world takes practice, just as it does in the inner world. Fear messaging doesn't come labelled and isn't easily spotted. It also doesn't exist in only one industry, or only on your TV. It is everywhere! I am not saying this to alarm or overwhelm you. Rather, I want you to be aware of it so that you do not give your power away to someone simply because of their profession or their good marketing.

Entire industries have been created purely to keep you permanently in the 'lolly aisle,' disconnected from your real purpose of being here and living from your authentic self. Industries and products that cater to your ego's sense of success have us lining up around the block. 'Quick fix' products fly off the shelf while lifestyle change solutions, permanent and lasting change advice and guidance, is more of a slow trickle. A dribble that many only come to once all other avenues have been exhausted and they are 'desperate.'

The most revolutionary changes occur in our lives when we no longer outsource our sense of worth, and we no longer give our power away. To set the tone in this way, I ask that you stop determining the merit of a product, message, or advice by who it's coming from and instead focus on how it makes you feel.

It's time to recognise that it's not only the beauty, entertainment, and fashion industries that market to your ego. The 'self-help' and health and wellbeing industries often do the same. There's plenty of 'spiritual' messaging that speaks to your sense of being flawed. Every time we 'bite' on this style of marketing, we are giving our power away to our own ego and to the collective ego. We are sending energy into the collective swirl with the message, "I am not enough."

It is our job, in our time here on this planet, to raise the vibration of the pot. We do this twofold: firstly, by creating a loving and kind inner world, and secondly, by being conscious of what we add to the collective pot. You are already well on your way with the first. However, you might only just be considering the second now. But that's okay because it is just an extension of what you have already been doing.

If you want to explore this intentionally, the first question to pose to yourself is, "What am I adding to the pot?" This requires you to be aware of the emotions, intentions, and energy that you are 'marinating' your contributions in. The second question is, "What am I doing with what I receive from the pot?" To do this, you need to be aware of how you respond to what life brings your way. When I say, "What life brings your way," I mean any experience that you have—be it an interaction with another person, the birth of a child, a change of job, a physical illness, the aging of your body, a change of seasons, the global economy, politics, or all that 2020 has brought your way . With literally anything you have encountered or could encounter, you have one of three ways to respond.

You can either add your reaction on top and send it back out, you can neutralise it, or you can transform it.

1. Adding on Top

If you encounter anger, and you respond with anger, you are adding your emotion on top, then flinging it back to the perpetrator (or an unsuspecting bystander). If you encounter fear and/or panic and it sets off your fear and panic, the pot now has more of those emotions in it than before you encountered the experience. Drama, abuse, and conflict can all be taken up a notch as we add our own on top of what we've encountered.

The media also encourages this adding on top. The MSM, and television in general, have for a long time now, been designed to appeal to our ego and its addiction to conflict and drama. If you aren't yet aware of this, just put the TV on and have a listen to how shows are advertised. There is generally a man's voice—deep, slow, and echoey, almost hypnotic—saying something like, "You won't believe this week's episode . . . all the tears, all the drama. Never have you seen anything like this before. It will leave you gripping the edge of your seat." And this could be advertising a *cooking show*!

The stronger our egos get, the more our society has been immersed in the growth of consumerism, escapism, and a disconnection from nature and each other. Our ego has become addicted to a steady diet of drama and conflict. And the media, along with many other industries, are well aware of this and using our fear to manipulate our decisions and our beliefs.

Watching these TV shows and adding our own feelings from our loungeroom is adding even more conflict and fear to the collective pot.

2. Neutralise It

The way to neutralise the energy of something you encounter is by not adding on top. You encounter anger, fear, conflict, abuse . . . and you decide, "This stops with me." You can do that by ending a conversation, turning off a show that is having a negative impact on you, or not responding to a comment on social media. Basically, the energy that has found its way to you moves on without being changed. The vibration of the pot, the quality, the level of fear and love, stay the same.

3. Transform Fear into Love

This is the highest form of the work you have come to the planet as a human to do. It is an act of love toward yourself, toward all of the planet's inhabitants, and toward Mother Earth herself. ACIM defines a miracle as a shift from fear to love. With this approach, as you consciously transform fear to love, you actively perform miracles.

Firstly, I must share with you that this is an act of compassion, not of suppression or disregard. When we encounter fear (and all the ways it presents itself, such as anger, doubt, jealousy, revenge, and violence), our own fear will most likely be triggered. Especially when we are just at the start of this work. The very first vital step is to pause and breathe. Recognising, honouring, and respecting our own reaction is critical in being able to transform it. It is really our inner world we are transforming, from a world of fear to one of love. When we take our fear by the hand, sit with it, and explore what it has to teach us in that moment, we regard our own pain, and we support our own experience.

Then we reassure our ego that we are the adult in the room, and we are in charge—this allows a shift over to our true guidance. We invite our Right Mind to transform our perceptions, our emotions, and our thoughts to ones that allow us to act from a place of love. Once again, this is an act of compassion. This does not ask you to be a martyr—in fact, quite the opposite.

We do not choose to transform the low-vibration energy we get from the pot, in spite of how we feel. Instead, we do it by honouring and taking responsibility for how we feel.

You are already doing this every time you are kind to yourself. Every time you choose to approach your fear gently, you are raising the vibration of the collective energy. It's so important that you understand that any work you do on yourself, and for yourself, benefits us all. We can only be as healthy as the sum of our parts.

The angry friend or stranger lashing out, the impatient driver on the road, the fear-mongering politician, the child having a meltdown, the system in which you don't feel heard, the industry that tells you are not enough, the parent that always nit-picks... I could go on and on. All of this appears to be outside of you. These are all examples of you receiving energy from the collective pot. It moves through one of us and onto the next person. As it does this, we each have a choice: do I add on top of it, do I neutralise it, or do I transform it?

Let's be honest. You won't always have the energy to transform it. You also won't always be 'awake' when an opportunity arises. Sometimes anger will come your way and activate the anger within you, and you will add a whole heap on top and shoot it out into the collective. That's okay; that's being human. But I want each of us to challenge the belief that this is power, that this is an example of our boundaries, that this is standing up for ourselves. Because in truth, this is nothing but a trigger, an unhealed aspect of ourselves, and an ego response. And in this way, nothing will ever change. We will continue to live in an ego-centric world, spinning from one drama to another.

So, when would you transform the fear you encounter to love? When you can—simply when you can. If we promise that we'll do it when we can, with eight billion of us, in any given moment of any given day, there will be enough people focused on love to significantly raise the energy of the pot. As the energy rises, the level and amount of fear that swirls around us all will significantly decrease. And it will become easier and easier for everyone to continue to practice this. With less fear in the pot, we consume more love at each 'meal,' and we become more and more connected and united. We start to see the best in each other. And we begin to allow for our humanness, while at the same time encouraging each other to rise into our fullness—to access our full power.

And this is what I wish for you, for me, for us all. May we continue to step into our full power, recognising that the only person who can truly keep us from it is ourselves. May we recognise the connection we have with each other and the vital part we all play in the transformation and evolution of this planet from ego to Right Mind—from disconnection and separation to unity consciousness.

As a result of reading this book, may you step out of limitation and see clearly what has been standing in the way of your expansion. May you step into your power with the trust and confidence that allows your higher self to create what you always envisioned you would when you chose to come here. May you, in all your fullness, set the tone of your life in such a way that it inspires and encourages all those around you. May you always remember who you are and the perfection of that.

Connected. Empowered. At Peace.

Remember these words, and you will always be brought back to these teachings—back to yourself.

Appendix

From Knowing To Doing –
The Practical Steps

If you are anything like me, you like to read through a book, do some of the exercises if you feel like it and skip some of them because you are in the flow of the content and don't want to stop reading. Thus, I have added this section with all the practical work in one place.

This way, if you have read through the book and now you want to do the exercises, either for the first time or more in depth, then here they are for you, all in one section. No need to go searching back through the book.

Also, an important reminder - short term relief comes from 'knowing,' lasting relief comes from 'doing.' This section highlights the 'doing', or the journaling exercises, throughout the book.

Set the Tone

Chapter 1 - Planting Seeds

*"Without realising who you are,
happiness cannot come to you."*

Yogi Bhajan.

Reminder

You are an incredibly powerful being and creator. You are an extension of all there is. You are equipped to create miracles and to transform anything, any experience that you find yourself in, and then use this as material to build yourself up. You have the ability within you to create a foundation that is so solid, so strong it can withstand anything without you losing your sense of self. An experience might make you wobble a bit. Still, with a foundation based on knowing who you are and feeling connected to all there is, and by making decisions from love rather than fear, you cannot be knocked down.

Affirmation

I always have the power. No one outside of me has any power over me.

Appendix

Chapter 2 - A Conscious Choice

"Hope and fear cannot occupy the same place.
Invite one to stay."

Dr. Maya Angelou.

Affirmation

Knowing that all of my thoughts, beliefs, and actions are fuelling either the fire of fear or the fire of love, I now consciously choose to fuel love.

Chapter 3 - The Power of the Pause

*"There are no circumstances around you more
powerful than the power within you."*

Iyanla Vanzant

To activate the power of the Pause:

- Breathe.

- Say to yourself, "I've got this." By doing so, you are letting Ego know that you are the adult in the room. From here on out, you will be choosing the responses to situations based on how you feel right now, the results you have been getting so far, and the results you want to have.

- Be gentle with your ego as it arises. It's only doing its job. It is simply responding the best way it knows how in order to keep you safe, and to keep itself safe.

- Respect your feelings at all times. Respect the reaction that has gotten through to the keeper. And simply begin to be more aware and more awake to the feeling of the difference between Ego and Right Mind, between Fear and Love.

Reminder

You have an Ego. Embrace it, learn to live with it, understand it, and factor it into your ongoing experience. Get rid of all thoughts of beating it into submission and start to lead it instead.

Appendix

Chapter 4 - Patterns and Programs –
It's a Family Thing.

"You cannot go back and change the
beginning, but you can start where you are
and change the ending."

C.S. Lewis

A reminder on the subconscious programming our ego receives during childhood

1). You are not a victim to this process.

2). You can become conscious of what is in your files, throw out what doesn't work for you, and 'update' them with new evidence. In this way, you can create new beliefs.

3). Your ego is only a tiny part of your mind. You have a whole other, potent part that can help you in this process.

4). This work is part of your purpose in this life. Whatever you help to 'upgrade' benefits the whole ancestral family lineage.

5). This is profoundly fundamental work for truly transforming your mind. You have just found the missing key to why, in the past, change hasn't been lasting.

Chapter 5 - Creating Space For Change

"To change yourself is an act of courage and wisdom. To change anyone else is impossible."

Martha Beck

This exercise enables you to access the programs and the unconscious patterning that your ego runs on.

So, let's proceed gently, knowing that this is an empowering activity. It can lead you to the freedom to be more authentically yourself, and to expand and evolve the way you live your life.

*The whole of Chapter Five is essentially the exercise, and to replicate it here in sections would possibly take it out of context and lose its power. So, whether you skipped the exercise as you were reading through or you are doing it for the second time, go back to start of the Chapter Five and refamiliarise yourself with the context. This will help you access all of the information you need to get the most out of this activity.

I highly recommend doing this exercise whenever you feel stuck on something or feel like a pattern just won't shift. By looking at what is still on file about the particular area you are working with, you will get powerful and freeing insight into what is in your way.

Appendix

Chapter 6 - Laying the Foundation

"As long as man stands in his own way,
everything seems to be in his way. "

Ralph Waldo Emerson

There are two fundamental lessons in creating change

A.   You can't attract what you aren't a match to, and

B.   You can't thrive in a hostile environment.

Question

If you could have one wish to transform how all of your relationships feel, what would you wish for?

Write the answer down in your journal and ask yourself – "Do I give this to myself?"

Remind yourself

Why should anyone else treat me better than I treat myself?

Question – "How am I treating myself?"

Use these prompts to find your answer –

- How do you feel about your emotions? How do you react to your sadness? Your anger or fear? When you cry, how do you feel about it?

- How do you speak to yourself when you are frightened?

- How you speak to yourself when you don't want to do something? How do you get yourself to do it?

- How do you speak to yourself when you make a mistake or get something wrong?

- What is your inner dialogue when you look at your body? When you are trying clothes on in a changing room?

- Do you ever swear at yourself or call yourself names?

- Do you praise yourself when you do something well?

- Can you list four of your own strengths?

- Are you able to receive compliments without feeling uncomfortable?

Appendix

Chapter 7 - Set The Tone

*"If you want people to love you,
love yourself and teach them how."*

Guru Singh

Fundamental Lesson

To BE that which you wish to experience in your life and to create an inner world in which you thrive, there are three fundamental things you need to learn to do:

- Recognise Ego.

- Separate YOURSELF from Ego.

- Pivot to your Right Mind/Inner Guide.

Recognising Ego/Fear

- Here are some feelings and other qualities of the experience of a fear (ego)-based thought:

- Tight, narrow, constricted

- You feel less than/not good enough.

- You are focused on, even obsessed, with detail.

- Focused on the problem. You can't seem to see or feel your way out

- Overwhelmed

- You feel inferior or superior.

- You feel alone.

155

- You feel like an impostor, as if any minute someone, or all of 'them,' will find out you have no idea what you are doing, or that you are incompetent.

- A need to be right and/or the good guy in any situation.

- Feeling like a victim.

- Powerless.

- Feeling or focusing on the separation between us all.

- Catastrophising / focusing on worst-case scenarios.

Initiating a shift from Ego to Right Mind

Grab your journal and jot down these prompts for when you recognise an ego thought:

- State 'Ego' or 'Fear' to remind yourself that you are separate from this.

- Say, "It's okay, I've got this. I'll take it from here." This lets your ego know that you are now in charge, you are the adult in the room.

- State, "We are not doing this," when ego tries to convince you of anything that is other than what you want to be feeling. For example, when it tries to convince you that your friend hasn't texted you back because she doesn't like you, or that you completely messed up the job interview you just had and the interviewers think you are an idiot, and so on and so on. We all know how this goes.

- Visualise a key in your mind whenever you hear something from your ego and grab it as a symbol of you taking your power back and getting back into the driver's seat of your own life.

Appendix

- State, "I will not use this against myself," to stop from beating yourself up with your insights, or when you find you're getting judgmental about your reactions or handling of a situation.

Recognising Right Mind/Love

Here are some feelings and qualities associated with the experience of hearing your Right Mind or Inner Guide:

- Open, calm, expansive.

- There is a focus on solutions and creative ways to solve 'problems.'

- Feeling empowered and inspired.

- Focusing on peace.

- Focusing on your heart's desires.

- You recognise how similar we all are to each other and how connected we are.

- You feel empathy and compassion for yourself, for all people and things.

- You can see the bigger picture regardless of the situation you are in.

- You feel confident and competent.

- Things seem beyond understanding. Often you don't know how you know what you know, or where the solutions or insight come from.

- You trust in the process of life and feel that everything will work out.

Chapter 8 - When The Critic Becomes The Guide

"You are the only one in the room whose narrative you need to pay attention to."

—**Matt Kahn.**

Definition of Boundaries

I will not use another's words or actions against myself, not even my ego's.

I will not use another's opinion of me against myself. Not even my ego's.

I will not use what society tells me about myself, against myself.

I am responsible for my inner world, and I decide what and who comes in.

The Lessons of the Trigger

Let's find some of your own gold. Grab your journal.

I want you to have a think about who has had, or still has, a large negative effect in your life. Whether or not they are still in your life doesn't matter. How long ago they had the impact also doesn't matter. Write down the names of anyone you can think of who has had a 'negative' effect in the way they made you feel, spoke to you, or treated you. Leave a few lines between each one.

Then, write a couple of sentences describing how they had a negative impact on you. What did they do? How did they make you feel? What negative or limiting beliefs did they set up in you? Spend as much time on this as you like. If a

Appendix

few lines are not enough, then continue onto another page. Write it all out until it feels like you are done.

Once you have completed this, turn to a new page and again write each of their names down on the page, leaving some space between each one. Now write the heading "My Teachers" at the top of the page. This time I would like you to spend a few minutes connecting with the opportunity that this person has provided to you. What did their words and/or behaviour help teach you that benefits you?

For example, they might have taught you to walk away from an unhealthy relationship, or maybe they taught you how competent you are, how independent you can be, or how strong and capable you are. Maybe they were the person who finally taught you to say, "no"? Maybe they were someone who taught you where your line is, and to recognise what is not acceptable for you. Maybe they gave you the opportunity to choose you, to recognise what you want—by showing you a whole lot of what you don't want?

This is not an exercise in forgiveness. Even if you still experience anger, sadness, or any other unresolved feelings, you can look for the lesson that is here for you. You can even take the person out of it, take all the details away, cross out the person's name, and ask, "What did I learn from this experience that serves me well?"

Now, this can get your ego alert and ready to take over with thoughts like, "I'll let you know what they taught me, they taught me not to trust anyone, not to be an idiot, not to be fooled and believe what people say . . ." Hmm, does that sound like information that builds you up or beats you up? Ego will use anything it can against you, hoping that it will stop you from being 'weak' and 'vulnerable' again in the future. Your Inner Guide, in contrast, wants you to build yourself up with anything you experience, and use what you learn as you navigate life to reach ever-greater levels of trust, compassion, and love for yourself and others.

Take some time to read over your list, genuinely connect in with your heart and ask, "What did I learn about myself that serves me well? That builds me up?"

Ground-breaking reminder

Your life is about you!

Appendix

Chapter 9 - Creating New Outcomes

*"A mind which is not crippled by memory
has real freedom".*

J. Krishnamurti

Creating Consciously – Moving beyond the details and allowing perfection to unfold. Creating in the flow

Grab you journal and have a think about what your values and priorities are. Feel into what you want to move toward. Write down as many as come to mind or heart.

Freedom? Family? Abundance? Spaciousness? Self- respect? Health? Empowerment? Love? Peace? Creativity. More time for _____ (reading, cooking, friends, quiet, art, dance?)

Pick one or two that feel the most appealing to you. (Starting with one might be the easiest until you become more comfortable and familiar with this process.)

Write down your priority and no other information. We don't need details. We don't need the why, the what, the how. Bringing in these kinds of questions will only move this whole exercise over to your Ego. Once you bring in details you bring in guilt and the need to justify.

Once you have chosen your value/priority to focus on write it down and circle it. This is now what all decisions and choices will be measured against.

This will now be your guide as you make decisions and choices in your daily life. You will be able to focus on your value/priority and ask, "Is this giving me more of this or less of this."

*For further info and context head to page 127

Chapter - 10 A Whole New World

"If you want to awaken all of humanity
then awaken all of yourself ...
Truly, the greatest gift you have to give is that of
your own self-transformation".

Lao Tzu

Question to regularly ask yourself

'Am I adding to the fear (feeding Ego) or the love (feeding Right Mind) on the planet?'

Be conscious of

"What am I adding to the pot?"

There are one of three ways to respond to anything that comes your way —

1). Add on top.

2). Neutralises it.

3). Transform fear to love.

Remember these words to come back to yourself

Connected. Empowered. At Peace.

Suggested Further Reading

» Anita Moorjani. *Dying To Be Me. My Journey From Cancer To Near Death, To True Healing.* Hay House Inc. 2012.

» Bruce Lipton PhD. *The Honeymoon Effect. The Science of Creating Heaven on Earth.* Hay House Inc. 2013.

» Eckhart Tolle. *Stillness Speaks. Whispers of Now.* Hodder & Stoughton. Ltd. 2003.

» Eckhart Tolle. *The Power of Now.* Hodder & Stoughton. Ltd. 1999.

» Esther and Jerry Hicks (The Teachings of Abraham). *Ask and It Is Given. Learning to Manifest Your Desires.* Hay House Inc. 2004

» Helen Schucman. *A Course In Miracles. Foundation For Inner Peace.* Penguin Group. 1999.

» J. Krishnamurti. *Freedom from the Known.* Rider. 2010.

» Pema Chodron. *The Places That Scare You.* A guide to fearlessness in difficult times. Element. 2003.

» Thich Nhat Hanh. *Peace Is Every Step.* Bantam Books. 1991.

» Wayne Dyer. *Wishes Fulfilled. Mastering The Art Of Manifesting.* Hay House Inc. 2012.

Printed in the USA
CPSIA information can be obtained
at www.ICGtesting.com
LVHW012121041023
760082LV00003B/152